A GLANCE BACKWARD AT FIFTEEN YEARS OF MISSIONARY LIFE IN NORTH INDIA

Published @ 2017 Trieste Publishing Pty Ltd

ISBN 9780649594054

A Glance Backward at Fifteen Years of Missionary Life in North India by Joseph Warren

Edited by Trieste Publishing Pty Ltd.
Cover @ 2017

www.triestepublishing.com

JOSEPH WARREN

A GLANCE BACKWARD AT FIFTEEN YEARS OF MISSIONARY LIFE IN NORTH INDIA

Trieste

PALANKEEN TRAVELLING.

A

GLANCE BACKWARD

AT

FIFTEEN YEARS OF MISSIONARY LIFE

IN

NORTH INDIA.

BY THE

REV. JOSEPH WARREN, D. D.

PHILADELPHIA:

PRESBYTERIAN BOARD OF PUBLICATION,
No. 265 CHESTNUT STREET.

1856.

NOTE.

SOUNDS OF LETTERS IN HINDUSTANI WORDS.

A, a, sounds like *u* in *butter*.
A′, á,   "   "   *a* in *father*.
Ch,   "   "   *ch* in church.
E, e,   "   "   *ai* in *pain*.
G, g,   "   "   *g* in *good*.
I, i,   "   "   *i* in *pin*.
I′, í,   "   "   *ee* in *seen*.
O, o   "   "   *o* in *note*.
Q, q, has the sound of *k* thrown back in the throat.
U, u, sounds like *u* in *pull*.
U′, ú,   "   "   *oo* in *fool*.
Ai,   "   "   *i* in *time*.
Au,   "   "   *ow* in *now*.

N. B. Some consonants have peculiar sounds, which cannot be imitated by mere readers, and it has not been thought worth while to mention them. Names of places, which have obtained a current orthography in English, have been written accordingly here, however incorrect. For instance *Benares*, correctly written, would be Banáras, in three syllables.

ERRATA.

Page 47, line 12, for *swarz* read *swarg*.
Page 59, line 3 from bottom, for *found* read *formed*.
Page 60, line 4, &c., for *kauda* read *kanda*.
Page 71, line 18, for *might had*, read *might have had*.
Page 78, line 5 from bottom, for *Bez* read *Beg*.

CONTENTS.

CHAPTER I.

INTRODUCTORY.

CHAPTER II.

HOUSE-KEEPING AND LEARNING THE LANGUAGES.

CHAPTER III.

THE PRINTING-HOUSE.

CHAPTER IV.

CATECHISTS: THEIR TRAINING, CHARACTER AND USEFULNESS.

CHAPTER V.

CHURCH BUILDINGS, AND PREACHING AT THE STATIONS.

CHAPTER VI.

ITINERATIONS.

CHAPTER VII.

THE PREPARATION OF BOOKS FOR THE PRESS.

CHAPTER VIII.

RELATIONS WITH EUROPEANS AND EAST INDIANS, AND THEIR INFLUENCE ON OUR WORK.

CHAPTER IX.

SUCCESS.

MISSIONARY LIFE IN NORTH INDIA.

CHAPTER I.

INTRODUCTORY.

In October, 1838, the reinforcement to our North India Mission, of which my family constituted a part, sailed from Philadelphia. At this distance from that time it is instructive to turn back and recall our feelings for a moment. Any one, who has left his native land for a prolonged residence abroad, if he were at all accustomed to reflection and feeling, must have felt vividly the uncertainty of his ever again mingling with the associates who had made the scenes of his early days dear to him. A missionary feels that it is highly probable that he will not live to see his friends again. The *wrench* given to his affections is most exquisite. Even if he be sure of a future visit to his country, he cannot but feel that he is to be separated from relatives, churches, fellow-students, society—all dear to him; and just when his social affections are warmest, and when he most feels the need of the aid to be derived from their proper indulgence. And if he has any proper sense of the magnitude and difficulty of the work to which he is going, his soul will be filled with trembling. The surviving members of our party will never forget the melting of

2

heart that we felt. Never did we feel so cut adrift
from the world; nor did we ever so really feel that
Christ was all to us. The first few days of our voyage were full of the contests of natural yearnings with
the workings of those higher feelings, motives and
principles that lay at the foundation of our going
forth. Never did Christ seem so precious to us as
when we had given all that we cared for to him.
When we do most for him, then we can most appropriate him; not from the idea that we deserve more,
but because we then come to feel more that we have
nothing but him.

Our party consisted of the Rev. James L. Scott and
Mrs. Scott, the Rev. John E. Freeman and Mrs.
Freeman, with Mrs. Warren and myself. Of this
party, Mrs. Scott and Mrs. Freeman, after several
years of great usefulness, are gone to a higher and a
better sphere. I will not refrain from the pleasure
of paying a deserved tribute to their worth. The
leading characteristic of Mrs. Scott was an energetic,
untiring spirit of enterprise. She was always ready
cheerfully to undertake any work by which she could
benefit the people, and promote the object of our mission. Mrs. Freeman was more known for great and
quiet gentleness—a gentleness that did not make her
influence less than that of the other lamented woman.
The females of the Allahabad mission church were
influenced by her to such an extent, that we may look
for the fruit of her labours to be reproduced, again
and again, in the future history of our Church in
India. Both of them were our dear friends; and both
left blanks in our circle that will not be filled in this
world. A list of friends may be lengthened—blanks
are rarely filled.

It would be useless to give an account of our voyage after such a lapse of time. The public is sufficiently acquainted both with such subjects, and with
the general impressions of missionaries on reaching

the country of their destination. The journey up the Ganges has also been described by others, so that it is not necessary to refer further to that. We will, therefore, pass over all these matters, and proceed, in the next chapter, to look at missionary experience in the field of actual operations.

The plan of this work is simple. It is to give specimens of all kinds of experience, both happy and sad; and to display all our ordinary modes of working, the reasons for them, and their results. The people and the circumstances, that affect our work, must be taken into view. The mode of doing this, which has been chosen, is to give a personal narrative of my own experience—not chronologically, but as to different subjects. My object is, to keep the individual out of sight, as far as the nature of the plan will permit; and on the thin thread of personal narrative to string anecdotes, sketches, and specimens, until the reader shall be able to gather an intelligible notion of our life and labours in India. An attempt is made to keep the reader from being wearied by the mere clanking of machinery, by interrupting and illustrating the narrative with all sorts of facts related to it. An additional chapter contains a brief sketch of the government of that country, and of different classes of persons, who are mentioned in the course of the work, so far as is necessary for the understanding of the narrative.

The object of the book is, to help the friends of missions to a full knowledge of the work, so that they may form just expectations, and be led to go forward with more interest in the matter, more earnestness of desire and purpose, and more hope, patience, and prayer.

CHAPTER II.

HOUSE-KEEPING AND LEARNING THE LANGUAGES.

AFTER reaching Allahabad we found that the Mission families were not in a position to keep us in their houses with any convenience to themselves or to us. A large bungalow had been taken for us and Mr. and Mrs. Freeman jointly. As Mrs. Freeman was ill, they could not join us in house-keeping immediately; and we therefore began by ourselves at once. While we had been tarrying at Benares, our boats had come on, and were unloaded the same day that we arrived. We spent the next day after our arrival, which was the Sabbath, at the house of one of our friends, and on Monday began our house-keeping.

As bungalows in Upper India differ considerably from descriptions of them in the Madras Presidency and Ceylon, which I have seen in books published in America, a description of the one in which we first lived, and of that which was afterwards bought for us, may be interesting. The one that was hired for our temporary use was much larger than missionaries need, or ever use in ordinary circumstances. It was situated nearly in the centre of a square lot of about six acres. A lane passing between two fields led to it from a retired road, so that the place was quiet and free from dust. In front of the house was a small parterre of flowering shrubs. The western part of the ground was a garden nearly filled with fruit trees. Along the north wall of the yard was a range of buildings—clay walls and tiled roofs—which contained the kitchen, stable, carriage-house, and about a dozen rooms intended as tenements for servants. The house faced the south. The entrance was a deep verandah, running the whole length of the

house, except that a small room was inclosed in each
end of it, used as lumber rooms, or places in which
the servants cleaned the lamps and performed similar
work for the house. The largest room of the house
was about thirty-five feet long, and twenty-two wide,
stretching along the front. At the ends of this room
were two smaller ones, serving as servants' hall, or
pantry, or for any temporary use; though in truth
their main office was to serve as passages to other
rooms, and to keep the heated outer walls as far as possible from the principal apartments. Behind this range
of rooms was another of three, of which the middle
one was largest. This room had no door opening into
the verandah on any side, but was entirely surrounded by other rooms. The light in it was consequently scanty, and the room gloomy, so that it
would be very rarely used, except in the very hottest
weather, when its distance from the external walls
would make it more cool than any other place in the
house. Back of these three rooms were two large
bed-rooms. The ends and back part of the house
were protected by verandahs; but the one in the rear
was enclosed and cut up into small rooms, to serve as
bathing rooms, &c. The house was of but one story,
and covered an enormous quantity of ground for
the amount of accommodation it afforded, compared
with houses in America. But it was intended to
accommodate but one ordinary family, and to keep
out the heat as much as possible. The roof was
pointed in the centre, very steep, and ran down low,
projecting out from the verandahs, so that the lower
edge of it was not more than nine feet from the
ground. It was of grass, and about nine inches
thick. The house presented scarcely anything but
roof to the view at a little distance: it suggested the
idea of a short stout person hidden by an enormous
and ungainly sun-bonnet.

The house that was bought for us shortly after,
2*

was much smaller, but in other respects very similar to the other. The roof was of the same form and material; the verandah completely surrounded the house, and bathing-rooms were formed in it at three corners. The rooms that it contained were—one of twenty-two feet by sixteen; at the end of this a pantry; and, back of these, two rooms of fifteen by sixteen feet each. This was too small to keep out the heat; and it not only afforded no accommodation for visitors, but was not sufficient for our family. After living in it some years, however, we were kindly allowed to add a sitting-room and study to this, which, with some minor alterations, made it a sufficiently good house.

The floors of bungalows are made of lime. The foundation of the house is first filled up with clay, which is well rammed down; then a course of broken bricks or *kankar* [limestone nodules] is laid over the clay and beaten down; then coarse lime mixed with small kankar is put on and very well beaten; then a plaster of finer lime is laid over all, and beaten lightly by a crowd of boys and girls for a long time, till, from being like a puddle of water, it becomes almost dry; and then it is finished off with a thin coating of pure white lime, not laid on like whitewash, but rubbed into the surface of the plaster, and carefully smoothed. Sugar, and various other articles, are incorporated with the two upper strata of this formation, to make the floor hard.

The ceiling of the rooms is cloth, tied to hooks over a cornice round the sides of the room, and supported by bamboos that run across the room. The cloth is white-washed; so that, when well put up, it closely resembles the plain lath and plaster ceilings in American houses. This cloth keeps scorpions, centipedes, and many other inconvenient things, from falling into the rooms, and upon whatever they contain.

The walls of these houses are made either of burnt bricks, or of those which are only sun-dried, or of clay in successive courses. All of them are plastered and whitened or coloured. The plaster is usually a preparation of lime, but is sometimes only clay and chopped straw. The walls, though clay, or laid up with clay mortar, stand well as long as protected from the rain; but if the white ants go up through the walls, and eat the thatch over them, as they often do, the first rain sends down a stream of water, which gutters the wall, and brings with it a load of clay into the rooms. The first rain that we saw in India caused us this awkward accident, in the hired house spoken of above. We sent for the agent of the house-owner, and showed him our trouble; but as we had nothing in that room to be spoiled, he laughed at us for considering the matter so sad and serious as we evidently did. A little straw thrust into the roof, and a little clay plaster applied to the wall, made all right for that season.

We lived about six weeks in the hired house, till our own was purchased. During this time we were struggling to learn how to speak to the people, and to understand the ways of house-keeping in that strange country. We could not have the kitchen in the house; the heat absolutely forbade that. Even the poorest natives do not kindle their fires for cooking inside their houses in the hot weather, but out of doors. We were, therefore obliged to keep servants. Many people in America may be astonished that we, who could have got on very well with one servant in America, should in India keep several.

A long detail of circumstances, to justify ourselves, will not be entered upon here; it is, or ought to be, sufficient to state simply that we were obliged to do so. We, having a fixed allowance, had quite as many inducements to lay up money as any clergyman's family in America; and missionaries, as a class, are no more likely to waste an income on servants for show than any other people. We should have been glad to live with fewer servants, and to have received a smaller fixed allowance from the Board of Foreign Missions, had it been practicable. But the exhausting climate, the necessary distance of the kitchen, the day-by-day mode of living there, the inveterate inefficiency of the servants, and the institution of caste, all combined to force us to have several servants, and still to be as badly served as a family in America is with one poor servant in their house. As to the last particular mentioned—caste—it operated in this way: the cook would not dust the furniture or sweep the house—it was against his caste. By this is not meant that there was any religious reason why he should not do these things—he could not be counted unclean for doing them; but the people of his caste had agreed that these things were low, and that they would not do them;—they are usually done by men of lower caste, and therefore they would persecute one of their own men if he did them. Again, the man that dusted the furniture would not sweep—it was beneath him; and the sweeper would not dust the furniture—he had never learned, and felt no need to learn, because he could get a living as a scavenger. Neither of them would bring water, for it was not their trade; and if we did not employ a regular water-carrier, every man about the place cried out, How are we to get water? Some years after our first settlement at Allahabad we had a boy from the orphan asylum to provide for. He was not a good boy, and could not be trusted in the printing-house, where there were opportunities to pilfer; but he was a nominal Christian, and it was our duty to give him employment and keep him under the means of grace if we could. We therefore made him water-carrier. We put a bucket and windlass to the well, and procured a yoke and pair of buckets for him. This made it easier for him to draw and carry water, than the Asiatic method, where it is usually drawn in a little, leaky, leathern bucket, by a small line drawn hand over hand, and carried in a goat-skin over the back. It also made it practicable for each person to draw for himself. But the complaints were loud and long. Nearly all our people, in the house and printing-house, refused to drink the water brought by a Christian—it was unholy; and to touch the bucket in the well, for the same reason. They represented to me, most pathetically, that I was putting them all to great inconvenience and expense. The native Christians did not join in these objections; but they had never seen or heard of such a thing before, and could not believe that it would work: they doubted the windlass, the buckets and the yoke; but above all they could not see how a Christian *could* be made a water-carrier; it was perfectly unprecedented. The support, therefore, that we obtained from them was small indeed; and even the lad employed looked on himself as put to a very strange use. He could not say that the employment was not respectable; for it has always been considered highly so. He could not plead that it was hard or unprofitable; but he knew that it was unusual, and that was enough to keep him from feeling easy in it. The experiment was continued, however, and worked pretty well, till the boy abandoned my place to try his fortune in Calcutta. One more thing may be said: as far as an opportunity to learn their feelings has been afforded to me, I am led to believe that our wives would prefer doing their own house-work in America to living as they do in India, were there not far higher and holier motives than personal ease to keep them there.

But to return from this digression. We had every thing to learn—language, facilities, customs, how to avoid being cheated, and how to escape doing wrong ourselves. Mrs. Warren, being still weak from her recent illness, required much of my assistance; and

the necessity of giving it was rather an advantage to
me at that time: a certain part of the language was
learned from necessity.   Much of the time was spent
in turning over an English and Hindustání dictionary,
to find out the names of things, and how to frame
certain phrases.   The dictionary was a most miserable
affair, often provokingly giving definitions out of
which nothing could be made, and often misleading
me by not properly distinguishing what are usually
called synonyms; but still we were led sometimes, as
well as misled, by it.   Our perplexities, with a cook
who did not know twenty words of English, and who
talked to us just as if we knew Hindustání, were often
most ludicrous.   We shall never forget the way in which
we learned the word *bhúl* (mistake); and will tell it as
a specimen of that which was occurring every hour.
We had bought a piece of mutton for dinner, and
handed it over to the cook.   After a time he came
running, with trouble in his countenance, and said he
had made a *bhúl;* adding a great deal more which I
did not at all understand.   The word *bhúl* completely
puzzled me; and, as it appeared that this must be the
key to his talk, I went into a diligent search of it in
the Hindustání dictionary, but lacked knowledge to
find the word from his pronunciation.   At last, after
long labour, I began to listen for other words, to serve
as starting points; and soon made out the words *kuttá*
(dog), *gosht* (meat), and *le gayá* (carried away), which
I knew before.   Thus it became apparent that he had
made the *bhúl* (blunder) of leaving the meat in the
kitchen unguarded, and a dog had carried away our
dinner.

The struggles which we constantly made to get
work done in the way in which we had been accustomed to have it done at home, were sometimes amusing, and sometimes distressing; and our success was
very small.   The little and numberless ways in which
the servants sought to cheat us, the dirty habits and

practices in which we detected them, and their childish helplessness in many things, all made us think, for
a time, that we should never be able to endure them.
But experience taught, and use reconciled, us at last.

After our own house was purchased we went into
it as soon as possible. The number and size of the
rooms I have already mentioned, as well as the general character of the house. This had one peculiarity.
Glass doors are generally considered a necessity. To
these venetians are added; or mats or quilted curtains
are hung up against the doors; and occasionally the
verandah is supplied with screens made from the stems
of a very thick grass, or split bamboos. The peculiarity of our house was, that it had the venetians, and
no glass doors: we could not have light without wind,
and its accompaniment of dust and heat. We carried
our little furniture into this house; and perhaps it was
better that the house was small. We had a tottering
teak-wood dining table; twelve Indian chairs of *tún*,
a wood resembling cherry; a rocking-chair, and two
painted chairs from Boston; a dressing-table and a
study table, which were the halves of an old round
table that I bought (too dear) for three dollars; a
cheap set of camp-drawers, wash-stand and boxes.
When furnishing ourselves with a bed in Calcutta we
had also bought a spare bed. We were told not to do
so; but our American notions of propriety were sadly
shocked at the idea of having no bed to offer a friend,
and we *would* buy it; but when we went into our
house we found that we had no place in which to put
the spare bed, and were obliged to sell it. We improved this furniture, and added to the number of articles, in the course of years, till we made our house
tolerably pleasant. We had few places to visit, and
our house was an important matter to us: we thought
it our duty to each other to do all we could to make it
a pleasant place to live in; and that our children
ought not to be brought up in unnecessary rus-

ticity.   This remark, however, is not intended as an
apology for anything like luxury: at no time while
we were in India would all our furniture, together
with horse and buggy, have been estimated at so much
as would have furnished some single chambers in this
country.

The floors were covered with coarse coloured cotton
cloth, printed in imitation of a carpet.   This cloth,
when first put down, looks rather gay, and in a hot climate is a good substitute for a carpet.   But it is soon
spoiled.   The day that we removed from the hired
house into our own, it rained violently for a short
time, and the wind drove the water across the verandah, and through the venetians, till it stood in puddles on Mrs. Warren's gayest new floor-cloth, which
cost $3.50 for the whole room.   A rustic candidate
for baptism, whom we had made watchman to give
him the means of living, was assisting us in moving
our goods, and Mrs. Warren found him churning the
colours out of the carpet in one of these puddles with
his naked feet.   The poor fellow stood trampling
away, and saying, in a tone of sorrow, " O see the
water ! we never can live here without glass doors !

The Mission thought so too; and accordingly we
began to make glass doors for the house.   For this
purpose we hired a carpenter, who worked in our
back verandah.   His mode of working, and some
anecdotes respecting his caste, will be interesting to
my readers, as specimens of the state of things in
that country.   His tools were very scanty, and of
the poorest quality.   Two small saws, two or three
chisels, a few bits, and a rod and string to turn
them, a small plane, and a kind of adze, which had to
do nearly all the work, with a few minor articles, are
the usual kit of a Hindustání carpenter and cabinet-
maker.   There are differences in workmen, but the
one I am describing was by no means the worst.
With his tools he spent more time in sawing out

one bit of timber than twenty similar ones would have taken up in America. His plane was so small and poor that nothing was made either quite smooth or straight. As much of his work as could possibly be done so, was done with the adze: he held a rough stick slanting before himself by resting it in a notch made in a block that lay on the ground; and he then hewed slowly, taking off mere bits of shavings, till he had brought it to the shape required. All his work was done sitting on the ground, except when it had to do with the door-frames already fixed in the wall. Pieces of wood, on which he was at work with both hands, were steadied by his toes. It was a great trial of patience to see him at work: he did nothing well; and yet he did exceedingly well when we consider his tools and education. He could not do in a month more than a carpenter with us does in three days: but then his pay for the month was not more than a good American carpenter gets for three days. He never made two things alike: our doors were of such peculiar sizes, though all nominally the same, that no one would fit another's frame; and no corner was a right angle, except by the merest accident. The rows of glass were far from running straight across the door, but were set up and down in anything but a fanciful manner. But after all, the doors kept out nearly all the wind they were intended to keep out.

This man (and he is but a specimen of his class) had a great propensity to sleeping, and a small amount of faithfulness. If he fancied that I was busy, he would lie down beside his work and sleep, when he ought to have been at work, and had already been absent more than the usual time. I did almost every imaginable thing to break him of the habit:—threatened him with his discharge and with fines; threw blocks of wood at him, taking care not to hit him, but wishing that he might think he had had

3

great escapes; and reasoned with him, so far as a
very scanty knowledge of his language permitted.
At last, in an evil hour, I thought I had discovered
an unexceptionable mode of awakening him, and
making him cautious for the future, at the same time
doing him no injury. He worked with only two
pieces of cloth on him—a dirty white piece wrapped
round his loins and tucked between his legs, and a
red piece wrapped round his head for a turban.
The weather was warm, and he was always bathing:
so I thought he could not be injured by water.
Accordingly the next time he was caught napping, I
went into the bathing-room, a door of which opened
into the verandah where he was lying, and threw a
wash-bowl full of water over him. He got up and
went about his work, after bathing at the well, and
I heard nothing of it for three or four days. Then
he came to me, saying, that he was in great trouble,
as his people had suspended him from caste privileges, and would neither eat nor drink with him.
The Hindustánís express these ideas by the phrase,
"To stop his pipe and water." A friend of his, a
great man of the caste, came to me to confirm the
story. They said that the caste, having heard of
the circumstance, presumed that the water had been
used, or at least touched by me, and was therefore
unholy; and that some of it had gone into his mouth;
though this he denied. They explained that, if the
unholy water only fell on his body, he would only
have to bathe in the river to be holy again; but if it
went into his mouth, he would have to fee the Bráhmans and feast the caste before he could be restored
to communion; and that this would cost about a hundred dollars, which I should have to pay. I learned
that it really was both law and usage, that if one by
any violence, or even by accident, injured any person's standing in his caste by producing ceremonial
pollution, he should pay all the expenses of his

restoration. They at first showed some signs of a purpose to insist that the water went into the man's mouth, in order to make me pay for a feast for them; and the man himself would have been willing that this should be the end of the business, had he not said before witnesses, in the first place, that his mouth had escaped the deluge, and thus furnished me with a ground of defence in a civil suit for damages. I stood out, of course, that I would not pay the money. At last the caste agreed to refer it to my honour; if I would say that I did not think the water went into his mouth, they would restore the man. As I fully believed the mouth had escaped, I said so; and that was the end of the business. This taught me to deal carefully with caste for all time to come.

Some years after this, when I had another carpenter, of another sub-division of the same caste, at work for the printing-house, he assisted me in making a bargain with some Bráhmans, who lived a few miles from the city of Allahabad, for some thatching grass for the bungalow. The price was settled at so much a thousand bundles, and eight or ten bundles were given by the Bráhmans, as specimens both of the thickness of bundle and length of grass which they were to give. These specimen bundles were carefully locked up in a store-room till they brought the grass. When they brought it, we found that not more than half of it was at all up to the specimens. These were produced, and I said that I could not pay the full price. I called some Hindús, who were engaged in the work of thatching the house, and were well acquainted with such matters, and asked them what was to be done. The Bráhmans agreed to leave the matter to them. They decided that I ought to pay about nine dollars less than the whole lot would amount to at the full price. This sum I deducted from the price, and paid the remainder. I was sure that I was doing them no wrong, but rather was paying them too

much. They murmured, and said they *would* have
the remainder—the full price agreed on at first. I
asked them why they brought me such grass—why
they gave such specimens if they did not intend to
bring grass to answer to them. They said bluntly,
that they had brought the specimens to induce me to
make the bargain; and then had given as good grass
as they could; that I must be foolish to expect to get
anything as good as the specimens given; and that
they had unloaded the grass in my yard, and *must*
have the money. I then told them they might go to
the civil court with the case, and I would pay whatever was decreed. They said no more to me. In a
short time the carpenter came to me, and said that
the Bráhmans were demanding the nine dollars from
him, on the ground that he had introduced them to
me, and assisted in making the bargain. I sent a
servant to order them out; but all the Hindús about
me joined in imploring that I would do no such thing
—something dreadful would happen after it. The
Bráhmans, they said, had agreed that if the carpenter
did not pay the money, one of them should rip himself up with a knife, and die on the carpenter's account. There were three of the Bráhmans, and they
had been overheard laying their plan behind a wall:
the youngest said that it belonged to him to die; but
the oldest said that he had lived a greater number of
years, and had eaten a great deal, and therefore he
ought to be the one. And so it was finally settled:
they were to make a formal demand, and use entrea-
ties, threats, and all other means short of a lawsuit;
and if the carpenter should hold out, the old man was
to kill himself on the spot, and *the carpenter would
have to bear the guilt.* No guilt so terrifies a Hindú
as causing the death of a Bráhman; and so confused
are the ideas of the uneducated Hindús as to different
kinds of causes, that they esteem the killing of themselves out of spite to another as the most exquisite

kind of revenge; because they fancy that all the
guilt of their death is, in this case, transferred to the
person on whom they may thus choose to lay it. The
carpenter was thoroughly frightened. He begged me
to give the money. I refused; and explained to him
and the Bráhmans, that if they chose to kill themselves in an attempt to extort money unjustly, they
alone would suffer for it. He then prayed that I
would lend him the amount. I refused again, because I thought it right to combat such mingled
knavery and superstition. But all this did not, as I
hoped it would, prevent the Bráhmans from carrying
out their purpose: they made a last solemn appeal to
the carpenter, with adjurations and curses, telling him
that they chose to practise upon him, because he believed in their power and doctrines, and I did not.
He broke down, borrowed the money, and paid them
the last farthing. He lost it: for I never would
pay it.

I will only add some anecdotes, that will do something to illustrate the matter of housekeeping in
India, and also the character of some classes of the
people.

Shortly after we were settled at Allahabad, we had
a cook, a Musalmán, and a low caste Hindú bearer,
as our house-servants. From time to time we missed
various articles of clothing, but supposed they might
have been mislaid during Mrs. Warren's illness, and
postponed the search for them till she should be
stronger. At length, when I had five hundred rupees, as treasurer of the Mission, in the house, and
was quite aware how much had been paid out of it, I
found the bag evidently too light; and on counting
the money, found that one hundred and thirty rupees
were wanting. The cook had no business in that
part of the house, and had never been seen there.
The bearer was the only person we could suspect.
Being entirely puzzled as to how to proceed, I called

3*

in the Thánádár. This is the head policeman of a
small district. The man, in whose district I lived,
appeared to be very shrewd. I thought, when he
winked at me, and told me he would find some clue to
the truth by his examination of the bearer, that his
shrewdness, and tact, and experience would certainly
be sufficient to find the money. On further examination of our goods it was found that half of my shirts and
many of our best articles of clothing were gone. This
was a sad loss, and we never recovered anything.
The Thánádár took away the bearer, and detained him
three days, but was obliged to discharge him, as he
could discover nothing on which to found a charge
before the magistrate. I afterwards learned, to my
great disgust and sorrow, that the Thánádár, during
this time, had miserably vexed and tortured the poor
man, in every mode that would not leave palpable
marks, in order to compel him to confess. The
bearer was turned out of our service, as we still believed him guilty, though we could not convict him.
In a week or two after this the cook asked for his discharge. I have forgotten the pretext, but that does
not signify—he left us. Immediately after this he
married a wife, though he already had one; and laid
out at least a hundred rupees on an enlargement of
his house, beside being known to live rather luxuri-
ously, though before he entered our service he was in
debt. Thus it became manifest to every one that he
was the thief; but still we could get no legal evidence
against him.

On this occasion my Munshí greatly regretted the
prevalence of English law and customs. He said that
under any native government the circumstances, which
were open to all, would be considered sufficient for a
conviction; and that it was perfectly ridiculous to
screen a manifest rogue because no one saw him take
the money. He asked, with much pertinence, Ought
the law to expect that a thief will take witnesses with

him when he goes to steal? He said, (and the natives often talk in this way,) that English procedure and customs as to evidence, are totally unsuited to Hindustán, and serve to screen offenders oftener than to punish them; and are precisely fitted to make a nefarious conspiracy against an innocent man completely successful. As an example of this evil, I may cite a case which occurred under my own observation.

A man was accused of having committed a burglary, aided by two friends, by breaking into a house and carrying off various articles, on Sunday, in broad day. The charge was proved by twenty-five witnesses, who all testified that they saw it, as they were sitting with the owner of the house. The assistant magistrate, a young man of very little experience, thought no case could be more clear; and he sentenced the supposed criminal to imprisonment with labour. The matter was brought before the judge by appeal; and he directed the discharge of the man on the simple ground that the more eye-witnesses there were pretended to be of such an act, the more improbable it became—that he could not believe the accuser, with twenty-five able-bodied men with him, would see his house broken open by any three men and not resist it; and neither would any three men perform such an act in such circumstances. The natives all praised this decision, and said this was all the weight that ought to be allowed to direct evidence, when circumstances were against its probability. Had the judge, as many would have done, considered every man's oath good who could not be convicted of perjury, the poor victim of a stupid conspiracy must have served out his time in prison. The accuser, the accused, and all the witnesses in this case were Mohammedans.

I ought to state, for my own good name, that after circumstances had shown that our bearer was not

the thief that I had supposed him to be, I exerted
myself to get him another place, and succeeded.

One of my principal employments during this first
summer was studying the language. The first teacher
proposed to me was Patthras, [Peter] a native Catechist. He came to me two or three days after my
arrival, introduced by one of the mission, and began
to talk to me in Hindustání, as if I knew it already.
I tried my very few words of his language, but we
got on badly. At length I managed to ask him how
he intended to make me understand him, as we had
no language in common. He answered in Hindustání, "by the dictionary." I did not understand the
word that meant dictionary; and after he had repeated
it many times, with many contortions and increasing
loudness of voice, as if emphasis would make me
understand, he mustered up his English and said,
"*dissenherry.*" I was so stupid that this was unintel-
ligible too, till he laid hold of the book, and told me
this was the *dissenherry*. I commenced reading the
gospel of Matthew with him; but we could not go on
together. His education had not been such as to
exercise his mind at all, and he could not explain anything; he was fat and gross, and a little labour or
heat put him almost out of his senses; and he was
never punctual, but always disappointing me and
making lame excuses. Beside this, I soon found that
it would not answer to lay myself under any obligation to him: he had already tried to borrow money
from me, and to get me to do various things for him,
which showed his greed most disagreeably. After
making an unsatisfactory beginning with him, it was
determined that I must have a better teacher; and it
was fortunate that this change was made so soon: for
I afterward discovered that he had allowed me to give
wrong sounds to certain peculiar letters, and wrong
accents, without correcting me; and in a short time

longer bad habits would have been formed, which it would have been very difficult to get rid of.

Patthras was by birth a Musalmán, of Lucknow. He had been a soldier, and held some inferior military office, in the service of the King of Oude, at Lucknow—the splendid and corrupt—the Paris of India. Perhaps a worse school for the education of a man could not be found in the world than employment about the court of Lucknow. The government is Mohammedan of the worst stamp; the people effeminate and vicious beyond all European imagination; offices are always bought, and the best part of their income is made up of bribes and the fruits of oppression. Every man in office preys upon those below him. The office that Patthras held under this government had a nominal pay of about fourteen dollars a month attached to it, which was often long in arrears; while he was married to two wives, and accustomed to some luxury and show. He had therefore become accustomed to cunning and rapacity, but was no worse than his fellows : probably was a fair average man for that place. Though I would not dare to say that he never was a Christian by conviction, yet it was evident that the leaven of his education remained, and continually fermented. As there is an English resident at Lucknow, to look after the interests of the East India Company's Government, and some assistants, besides some English and East India people in business, the Company keeps a chaplain and surgeon there. Patthras became acquainted with some of these, and was led to examine Christianity. The chaplain took him under instruction; and, after he had separated from one of his wives, settling some little landed property on her, he baptized him. Thus he stripped himself of his little hereditary estate, parted with a wife of whom he always professed to be fond, and lost his commission in the army. He was looked upon at the time as quite a martyr; and far be it from me to say that it was all rascality: he may have been sincere. But his latter course laid him open to the shafts of suspicion: it could be said that he had experienced the evils of bigamy, and was willing to give up one wife in order to live in peace with the other; that his land was not sufficient to support his family, and brought him little or nothing when he could not personally superintend it, and so was no sacrifice when given up; and that he hoped to be petted and made great by the English, which would more than compensate for the loss of his office. It could also be supposed that he was one who sincerely took up with the truth, but when called to suffer for it, was offended. His old corrupt education and habits, at any rate, resumed their influence. He became first luxurious again, and got in debt; then, when dunned by his creditors, he made rapacious demands of his employers; then cunning and falsehood, those invariable resorts of the weak and slavish, were taken up again; then rage against us, for not satisfying his cupidity came on; and finally apostasy, or playing fast and loose with both Christianity and Islám, was the last scene of his history with which I became acquainted.

But it must not be supposed that Patthras was suffered to go to ruin in this way without the most strenuous efforts on our part to preserve him from a fall. He had been taken up by two gentlemen at Allahabad, who paid his whole wages, and set him to work under our Mission, and in the especial charge of Mr. Morrison. These gentlemen gave him an income that secured him and his family a better living than nine out of ten families of the same rank in Hindustán have; and they looked after him diligently, gave him advice and encouragement, and befriended him in every possible way. They once paid his debts, and cleared him of all his difficulties, on his promise to live within his income for the future, and to ask no

more similar favours. When he again got into the
same kind of difficulties, and to a greater extent, Mr.
Morrison fully relieved him, after pitying him,
instructing him, and doing everything that the largest
interpretation of Christian obligation could demand.
Patthras, as before, promised everything, but went
on in the same course worse and worse. His creditors
at length pressed him again. He promised falsely,
and equivocated. He thought us severe, and told
several persons of his troubles. The Episcopal chaplain of the station, a good but weak man, thought he
could manage him, and we consented that he should
try. His two friends agreed to pay his salary into
the chaplain's hands, and he agreed rigidly to see
that Patthras's necessities were cared for, and to pay
all that could be saved monthly to his creditors.
Patthras consented to this arrangement; but before
a week was over declared, quite falsely, that the
chaplain was literally starving him. He told me
such a pitiful story that I gave him some money; and
when the chaplain heard of it, he was much offended
at me for believing any part of the story. Patthras
then quarrelled with the chaplain; and about the
same time came to me again, apparently labouring
under all the excitement of a madman. He showed
me the passage in the Acts of the Apostles about the
community of goods; he accused me of not obeying
the command of Christ, in that I did not share my
goods with him; he said that I saw him having need,
and shut up my bowels against him. I treated his
fanatical notions with all the forbearance that was
possible, and calmly taught him what was right.
When I explained to him that I did not think he had
need, according to the sense of those words as used
by the Apostle John, he became so thorougly enraged
that the foam gathered on his lips. He said he could
listen to a man no more, who could give such a selfish
interpretation to Scripture; and when asked if his

own interpretation was not as liable to be considered selfish, he took a sudden and angry leave of me. A few days afterward he pretended some business at Lucknow, and got a fortnight's leave of absence from his employers, and never returned.

This circumstance, coming as it did in the early part of my missionary life, distressed me greatly. And even now I cannot think of the case without sincere grief. The poor man must have been a most desperate hypocrite all the time; or have fallen into snares of the wicked one, that ought to excite our deepest pity. Whatever view we take of his case, it is one that causes sorrow.

After Patthras ceased to be my Munshí, as a teacher of languages is usually called there, I engaged an elderly man, who had been the Munshí of many gentlemen. He was a Musalmán, learned in Persian and Hindustání, and thought himself learned in many other things. He had various quips of logic, that he thought most profound and valuable; and fervently believed many most monstrous fables about natural history and science, that were vastly amusing. He was pliable, affable, polite, quick, shrewd, and very conversable. With his private character I had, of course, nothing to do, even though it could not be considered a matter of indifference to me; but there was no reason to suppose it very estimable. All that I know about it with any certainty is, that he was an opium-eater, and showed in his conversation a great deal of unscrupulousness as to morals, while vaunting highly his honourable principles. With this man I continued the reading of the gospel, and began that of some native works of fiction, which are thought most useful for teaching one the idiom of the language; but the greatest advantage was derived from talking with him. I undertook to teach him Christianity, and our conversations on this subject were long and interesting. He helped me to words. He

had acquired a perfectly wonderful faculty of seeing
what word his pupil wanted, and would turn it up in
the dictionary, and tell how to fit it into the sentence
that was being framed, without at all interrupting the
train of the conversation. Then he made me tell him
long stories about railroads, telegraphs, electricity,
chemistry, governments and customs in Europe and
America, and "Nupaloon Boniparty," whom he
thought almost a greater man than Alexander the
Great—a decided stretch of belief for an oriental; for
Alexander is the only person in Ancient History,
having a connection with Europe, of whom the orientals now know anything, save as such knowledge is
newly introduced along with English education. The
Munshí sometimes told me tales, watching my countenance to see where he needed to explain more fully.
He set me right about the pronunciation of difficult
letters, and advised me to walk up and down the verandah practising. Accordingly hours on hours were
spent in this peculiar exercise—an excellent mode,
amongst others, of acquiring a correct enunciation
and intonation. After a few months passed in this
way, I was obliged to discharge this man, in order to
unite with Mr. Freeman in hiring one man between
us both, from motives of economy. This man was a
good teacher also; and, after ceasing to be Mr. Freeman's teacher, for many years was attached to the
printing-house as Munshí and proof-reader; and, of
course, he continued to give me occasional assistance
in the language. This was a considerable advantage.
We may well doubt whether there is not often an unwise economy practised as to the expense of language
teachers for missionaries. It is customary to discharge them as soon as they *can* be dispensed with,
when it would be much better, in many cases, to retain their services for several years: the missionary's
preaching and writing would often be incalculably the
better for it, if he have a talent for language worth

4

cultivating at all.　A man has *not* learned to speak a
foreign language when he can tell in English the
meaning of what he reads and hears, and can be understood when he speaks: there is something beyond
all this.　To speak effectively he must gain the power
of speaking like a fluent native.　A great deal of
practice, and a scholarly companion to guide him, are
both necessary to the missionary for this end.

The Munshí last referred to was a much more se-
date man than the former one; he was even severely
formal in his outward manner.　He was very devout
and religious, and expressed so much concern to arrive at all that was true, that I often had great hope
that he would be converted to Christianity.　This
hope was, for a long time, encouraged by his whole
manner.　He was mild and reasonable in discussions
of religious points, and seemed deeply impressed with
a conviction of certain deficiencies in the Mohammedan system.　He often shed tears in our conversations
when the love of Christ was set forth; and once told
me that the Christian scheme of salvation was beautiful, perfect, and entirely worthy of God.　But I at
last discovered, with intense pain, that two things
hindered his conversion.　The first was spiritual
pride: he could not be persuaded that he was not
quite pious and righteous already.　His zeal, devotion,
and religious reputation were as great hinderances to
his practically coming to the light, as open and outrageous vice can ever be.　The second hinderance was
his love of women: Christian practice in this respect
was not at all to his taste; and the license allowed by
Islám was highly so.　There was something extremely
odd and disgusting in his sanctified appearance and
his lasciviousness taken together; but he was probably unable to perceive their incongruity.　A pretty
widow, whom he had kept in his house for some time,
on the footing of supplementary wife, ran away with
all the family jewels.　He came to me with the de-

tails of her crime, suffering great shame and vexation.
I pointed out to him that this could not have happened had his domestic relations been on the Christian
plan, and told him that sin brought sorrow. He said
he had not been sinning: he had taken the woman to
keep her from being ruined by some bad fellows.
"And her living with you was not the same kind of
ruin?" He made no reply. Now I am quite aware
that this account of my teacher may seem indelicate
to some people. But I reply, to any such objection,
that my object is to show the people and the character and operation of their religious notions; and that
this cannot be done in any better way. I have mentioned above a transaction that was considered perfectly allowable and respectable by the society in
which the Munshí moved.

During this year our friend, the Rev. James Wilson, was living not far from us. He was four years
my senior as a missionary, and preached in Hindustání with considerable ease. He had a Hindustání
service in a room where the orphan girls' school was
taught. This service was regularly attended by me,
partly for the sake of example, and partly to learn
the language. This was of great advantage to me;
for though at first I understood nothing, very soon
some phrases became known; then others; then
many words, which I did not understand, were looked
up in the dictionary; idioms were noticed: in short,
a sort of preaching dialect became familiar to me,
and assisted me in a way that the books I was reading would not have done. In the course of this
season Mr. Wilson baptized an elderly Musalmán
woman. This was the first baptism of a native that
I had seen, and I was greatly encouraged by it.
My memory now goes back to this and some other
occasions, and fixes upon them, as luminous points,
with great joy. This first baptism; the first Hindustání communion at Allahabad; the opening of the

church that we built there; the finishing of the buildings for the printing-house; the completion of the
fund for buying our school-houses at Agra; and
several other occurrences, show me that I have much
to be thankful for.

My studies during this first summer were much
interrupted by the sickness of Mrs. Warren. We
were at one time afraid that her health would not
endure the climate of India, even if she should survive the first summer. But it pleased God to restore
her, and still to spare her to return to America with
me, after an absence of nearly sixteen years. Her
illness was caused, no doubt, partly by the exposures
of our journey, and by her sorrows; but I may as
well state, for the warning of all who may be in a
position to profit by it, that it probably was also
caused by our mode of living during the early part of
that summer. We had been obliged to contract a
debt to the full amount of the price of a horse and
buggy, and our furniture was most scanty. We
therefore determined to live in the practice of the
most severe economy; and kept the table as low
as possible, and avoided the employment of men
for the *tattí* and *pankhá*. The tattí is a thin screen
made of the fragrant root of a grass, and is used in
a door, where, wetted frequently, it causes coolness
in the house by the evaporation of the water, which
is very rapid when the hot wind is blowing. The
pankhá is a large fan, usually hung in all India rooms,
and swung by a rope that runs through the wall.
The agitation of the air caused by it is very refreshing. These two means of mitigating the heat are
universally resorted to by all Europeans in Upper
India, where the heat is much greater than near
Madras or Bombay, though the latitude is higher.
The Government furnishes these articles in the bar-
racks of European regiments; and this fact proves
that they cannot be considered luxuries, but rather

necessaries. The expense is not very great, because unskilled labour is exceedingly cheap there; but we thought it our duty to save it. This economy was unwise, because injurious. The medical man at length peremptorily ordered us to resort to the pankhá.

It may very likely occur to some reader to say, in substance, "How much better it would be if missionaries would go out unmarried! See how much unhappiness, and even hinderance to this writer's proper work, resulted from his having encumbered himself with a wife." If this objection to the marriage of missionaries possessed no force, it would not be worth while to answer, or even refer to it: it is just because it contains truth that it ought to be answered. Nothing is gained by taking up ultra-positions; therefore let it be confessed that there may be men and circumstances such as to make celibacy desirable. But generally, and especially in India, it is better that a missionary should be married. All the ordinary arguments in favour of the marriage of the clergy apply in the case of the missionary, and these it is not necessary to repeat. All the special objections to the marriage of missionaries, who are going to barbarous places, fail of their force, in a great degree, when applied to India; because there medical assistance can usually be procured, and we live under a regular system of laws duly administered.

The special reasons why a missionary to India ought to be married are as follows:—Our work there is regular, not admitting of much excitement, and often involves great trials of faith and patience. A missionary is often isolated from general society to a great extent; and if he have occasional invitations to the houses of English residents and fellow missionaries, they can occupy but comparatively little of his time, leaving him generally the sole occupant of his house. If, in these circumstances, he becomes listless, languid and melancholy, there is not much

4*

cause for wonder. It would be no small advantage to have his family about him, to produce a change in his ideas and feelings; and a good wife would incite him to keep on in patience and hope. The amount of the gentlemen's labour that ought thus to be carried to the credit of their ladies, no stranger to our work can conceive. It is true that now and then a sick wife causes the return of a missionary from the field; but I am confident that if it were a matter that could be sifted by an impartial person, he would find that many married men remain in the field vastly longer than they would have done if unmarried; and that more men leave the work because they *are not* married, than because they *are*. I have known several bachelor missionaries, and have no hesitation in saying that, with a few happy exceptions, they were sickly, did not settle to their work well, and were not able to preserve that suavity which was necessary to their own and their associates' comfort; and, when some of them were afterwards married, they proved to be as hearty, steady, industrious and agreeable as any men. Some of these statements may be doubted, and the arguments may produce a smile; but being deeply conscious that in them I am uttering great truths—indeed, that their greatness is exactly in proportion to their homeliness—I shall not be deterred from saying them. A second special reason for our being married is, that a single man cannot deal with the native Christian women as it is desirable to do. A wife's influence, example and instructions are requisite. What could I have done towards advising young girls from the orphan asylum, when first married to very young men in the printing-house? Every person of any reflection can perceive how important it was to our new community that a woman should aid in forming it. Another fact, to show that a lady should be present, is the absence of any proper sense of the value of chastity amongst the people. Even the native Christian women do not feel on this matter as American women do. The civilized ideas that have made unchasteness a special sin and loss of honour, have yet to grow up there as a product of mature Christianity; at present it is no more than any other transgression of the law in their estimation. This fact makes it peculiarly necessary that a Christian lady should be amongst them, to aid by her example and her precepts in forming a proper sentiment on such subjects. A gentleman might, indeed, preach all that need to be said about this subject; but no one but the missionary's wife can exert that undefined, often unrecognized, but most important influence that always, as it were, floats around, and is diffused by the true Christian woman—for, if the missionary is not married, no lady will be so situated as to exert this influence upon his people. And the absence of proper ideas, which is here referred to, places the unmarried missionary in danger. This, however, is a part of the subject to which I will only allude. Still another reason why missionaries should be married is, that the natives usually take it for granted that all single men are unchaste. They know so much of their own desperate corruption, that they consider purity impossible.

CHAPTER III.

THE PRINTING-HOUSE.

WHEN it was arranged that Allahabad should be my station, it was determined that advantage should be taken of my knowledge of the printing business to set up a press there. In the course of the history of this undertaking the reasons for it will sufficiently appear; and therefore it is not necessary to set them out formally here. This plan suited my tastes in some respects: I was fond of the press, and of that class of undertakings that are connected with it. It had been my intention once to make my way in the world as editor and publisher of a newspaper; and this intention had been laid aside when an overpowering sense of duty made me seek the ministerial office. Now, when something like my old propensity could be gratified along with the employments of my new calling, the prospect was very pleasing to me. I do not, on the whole, regret my course in this respect; though I at length became thoroughly weary of the amount of secular business that was involved in it. I still believe that the press was as important to our operations at that time as I thought it to be, and but little less so now; and that carrying it on is a business most honourable and useful; but the desire to preach and translate more than that employment allowed me time to do, induced me, two years before leaving India, to turn over the place to my successor very gladly. The Rev. L. G. Hay of Indiana, who was sent out to relieve me at my request, has charge of the press now.

A medium iron press, three kinds of English type, and a considerable quantity of printing paper, were sent out with us. These went, with our baggage, to Allahabad by boat. It would have been well if I had remained in Calcutta some time, to learn the ways of Indian printing-houses, to find out what was wanting in my apparatus, to remedy defects where there were workmen accustomed to such things, and to learn from our friends up the country what kind of work we should have to do, so that the necessary kinds of oriental type and workmen could be engaged at once. But a complete want of experience in these respects prevented all parties from knowing what to do.

When we arrived at Benares we found that the missionaries of the Church of England and of the London Missionary Society, with some other friends of the cause, had formed a Tract Society, or were about to do so; and that, because there was no printing establishment that could at all do their work nearer than Calcutta on the one side (four hundred and twenty-five miles), and Lodiana on the other (nearly seven hundred miles), they had intended to set up a press for themselves, and as a beginning had bought a Persian and a Nágarí fount of type. But they were encompassed with difficulties: they had amongst them no one who possessed any of the mechanical experience that was requisite, and there were no workmen within their reach; the engagements of all the missionaries were such that no one could be found to take that efficient charge of the affair that alone could render it successful; they had neither press nor buildings; and above all, they had no money —the income which they expected their society to have, being by no means adequate to such an undertaking; for these reasons they proposed to me to buy their type, and thus enable them to give up their plan; and, as the type was what we should certainly require, we agreed to take if off their hands. This Benares movement is mentioned merely to show that such a press as ours was wanted in that region. At that time, beside our Mission press at Lodiana, there were only two presses in all the region north and west of Calcutta, and these were principally engaged in printing two English newspapers at Delhi and Agra. Since the establishment of ours a large mission press has grown up at Mirzapore, a very large one at Agra, a small private one at the same place, a large newspaper establishment at Meerut, since removed to Agra, another large newspaper and job press at Lahor, and a smaller one at Benares. Beside these, little lithographic presses have sprung up all over the country in great numbers, for printing Urdú and Persian books. These grow up like mushrooms, and often fail like them too. About two

years since there were seven at Agra alone. Notwithstanding this great increase of presses, ours has
experienced no lack of work. This certainly shows
that our press was needed when established; and it
also exhibits a great and gratifying improvement of
the country in some respects.

The languages and dialects in which we had to
work, may as well be mentioned here, in order that
future allusions to them may be easily understood.

The language of Upper India is divided into two
dialects, having mainly the same grammar. Sometimes these dialects are distinguished as the *Hindustáni* and the *Hindúí*, or *Hindí*. By these terms it
was probably intended to make the *first* as belonging
to the country at large, that is, to *Hindustán;* and
the *second* as being proper to the branch of the people called *Hindús*. In these senses the terms are not
inappropriate; for the Hindustání is a sort of *lingua
franca*—a language spoken more or less all over the
country; and the Hindúí is nearly confined to the
Hindús of the north-west. But the more general dialect is more exactly designated by the term *Urdú*,
which means *the Camp*, indicating the origin of it in
the camp of the Persian-speaking invaders of India,
where it was formed on the pure Hindúí or Hindí.
From the north-west it has been carried all over
India, wherever the Musalmán power extended. But
the north-west remained its main field, and it has
retained its beauty and power chiefly there; or rather
has been more cultivated there, because this was the
chief seat of the Musalmán dominion. In this work,
whenever I speak of these dialects in general terms,
not intending to distinguish one in particular, I shall
use the term *Hindustání;* but when the reference is
to either especially, the terms *Urdú* and *Hindí* will
be used. The difference between these two dialects
consists mainly in the different sources from which
their substantives were derived. In both of them the

verbs and the particles, and the grammatical construction and forms are very nearly the same; but the Urdú takes the greater part of its nouns from the Persian and Arabic, while the greater part of those employed in the Hindí are either indigenous or Sanscrit. Some, of course, are common to both. In addition to this, however, the Urdú often employs Persian constructions by way of ornament. A sentence, given in both dialects, will illustrate the peculiarity as to substantives:

Urdú—Ai hamáre Báp, jo *ásmán* par hai!

Hindí—Háe hamáre Pitá, jo swarz par hai!

English—O our Father, who heaven in art!

The alphabet generally used for the Urdú is the Persian or Arabic character. In common parlance there is a distinction made between the Arabic and Persian letters, though they are identical in principle, the latter being only a more flowing and more easily written form of the Arabic. This character is very round and stiff; while the Persian indulges in more elongated strokes and more flourishing tails. In the Persian also, as being the character for ordinary writing, the forms of some of the letters are simplified a little. In Hindustán the Persian character is much more easily read, from its more constant employment in writing, than the Arabic, though the latter is much more plain; and towards Lodiana the people say they cannot read the Arabic at all. It is highly desirable to use the Arabic character in printing, instead of the Persian, whenever it is possible. The Arabic *joins* with tolerable ease; but the forms that have been given to the same letters, in the Persian mode of writing, are such that it is impossible to join them in a straight line, and we are obliged to have compound characters, of two, three, and even four letters, cast together, in order to join them in the manner of manuscript, without doing which they would look badly, and offend the eye, by being against all rule. Ordinary readers may get a better idea of this matter when I state, that with three hundred boxes in a type-case we can print Arabic very well; and that my first fount of Persian letter had over eleven hundred, and was still very imperfect. Printers will sympathize with me when I tell them, that the *kerns*, or letters that stood partly off the body of the type, were almost half of the whole number. These kerns project above and below the body, as well as on both sides. After a form went to press they were continually breaking down, leaving letters headless, or tailless, or without distinguishing marks, thus frequently changing one letter into another, and making a serious error. On one occasion, in printing the Book of Proverbs, the breaking of a slender initial letter made us say, "In the multitude of *lions** there is safety"—instead of *counsellors*. This character is also a very wasteful one for printing: the lines have to be put at such a distance from each other, that a small book becomes a large one. For these reasons we always use the pure Arabic style of letter when we can. But, as this is very disagreeable to native readers, many efforts are made to do printing in the Persian letter. Lithography has been resorted to, and many books and tracts have been printed by it. This is more expensive than letter-press, and can never be an efficient substitute for it, except for tables, &c., and works of which but few copies are wanted.

Further, the Persian and Arabic characters are both unfit for printing, because they contain no full system of vowels. They may be vowel-pointed like Hebrew, but this is so expensive that it will never be practised for common works. As a specimen of the difficulties that assail a student using this character

---

* My Munshí thought this was all right enough. He said he supposed that Solomon had learned that the lions would politely wait for each other, so that the man would have time to escape!

without vowel points, let us take a word of three radicals, say, *z l m*—forming a word in common use—*zulm*. This may be read zalm, zalam, zalum, zalim, zilm, zilim, zilam, zilum, zulm, zulam, zulum, zulim. Most other words of three radicals may have all these pronunciations. Of course, use commonly enables us to perceive what a word really is; but it frequently happens that a reader cannot tell what the word is, till he has looked onward through the sentence, and learned it from the connection; and thus he sometimes has to go back and correct the pronunciation. For this reason no readers are fluent save those who have had a great deal of practice; and it is usually a work of great difficulty to teach a boy to read even tolerably well.

These difficulties had been felt before my arrival in India, and had caused many to adopt the plan of writing Urdú in the Roman character. Some diacritical marks were adopted, that made this alphabet one of the most perfect that has ever been used. These marks, so far as they can be made intelligible to persons who are not acquainted with that language, are used in this work.

The great reasons for using this adaptation of the Roman alphabet are—first, its economy of space ; no crowding will bring any native character used in India, into the same compass that this occupies. Printed in the smallest Arabic or Deo Nágrí letters the Bible occupies two large octavo volumes ; while it may easily be put into a little more than half the same space in a good, fair Roman letter—and, if crowded as many English editions are, it need be no larger than they are. I once made a calculation of the expense of printing and binding five thousand Bibles in the Urdú dialect, in two different ways. It was proposed to print this number—one thousand of which were required for the use of native Christians, who could, with very few exceptions, use the Roman character, and four thousand were intended for distribution to other natives. These four thousand must be printed in the native character. It was thought by some that as there was to be an edition in the native character at any rate, we could not afford the expense of another in the Roman; but my calculation showed that the paper, binding and press-work, that would be saved by putting one thousand in the Roman character, would more than pay for setting up the type and reading the proofs of the extra edition. This calculation did not include the saving that would be made in the expense of transportation—not a small matter in such, and so large, a country.

The second reason is, that there is, as already intimated, greater certainty of readily perceiving the meaning of that which is read. This mode of writing was promoted by Mr. Trevelyan of the Civil Service, by Dr. Duff, and by many others; but still it has met with most unworthy opposition. Some learned men disliked any change. There is a spirit of conservatism in many excellent English minds, that seems to partake more of the nature of an instinct than of a product of reason. This conservatism is, no doubt, highly useful in many cases; but it quite as often stands stupidly in the way of improvement. These men were supported by a host of others, some of whom were not learned, but desired to appear so, and therefore affected to despise the simpler and more certain alphabet, as if it were only a crutch for ignorance and imbecility. Others had been accustomed to spelling native words and names, when they had occasion to use them in writing English, with vowels according to the English sound; and were therefore opposed to the sounds of the vowels in the proposed adaptation of the Roman alphabet, which were continental. It was in vain to show them that the greatest of their own grammarians, Sir William Jones, and the greatest of the authors of oriental dictionaries, Shakspeare and Yates, used this alphabet—it was enough that they were asked to adopt a new use of the vowels —they could see no reason for it. In the face of such an opposition the reform has made slow progress, but it has not been abandoned. It is to be hoped that all Christians will learn to use this alphabet, so that books prepared expressly for them may not need to be put into the vastly more expensive shape; and it is certain that all such books are easily used by natives educated in English, whether Christians or not. In this way this alphabet will supplant the others by degrees, till the country is at last delivered from their burden. It will also tend to throw into the shade impure and mischievous native books. Beside definiteness and certainty in spelling, the Roman character also affords the opportunity to use capitals and italics, both which are entirely wanting in the native alphabets, as well as punctuation. Of course we cannot print tracts for promiscuous distribution in this character, as we must furnish the natives with that which they can read.

The Hindí dialect is usually written and printed in the Deva (or Deo) Nágarí, the Sanscrit character. This is a square, bold letter, and very much better for printing than the Persian, though its vowels are placed above and below the line, and are troublesome; and it is too cumbrous for economical printing. Still it is plain, its vowel system nearly complete, and its general appearance good. Its chief characteristic is, that it is written under a heavy straight mark drawn along the top of the word, so that the letters seem to hang down from the line, as if strung upon it.

There is a simplification of the Nágarí alphabet, called the *Kaithí*, which is much used in some parts of the country. It is similar in form to the Nágarí, rather more expensive in printing, less definite in expressing sounds, and less beautiful; but it is very desirable to use it in some places, because it is more extensively read. We were, therefore, obliged to have this letter, as well as those before named, in our printing-house.

From this it will be perceived that we were obliged to have three kinds of type for printing the Urdú dialect—the Persian, the Arabic and the Roman. For the Sanscrit language and the Hindí dialect we have the Nágarí and the Kaithí. Then English work had also to be provided for. All this caused the labour and care of commencing such an establishment to be very great. The work that a missionary has to perform in qualifying himself to use, and to superintend any kind of operations, in so many characters and dialects, is also not small.

Shortly after our arrival at Allahabad, a friend, E. G. Fraser, Esq., assistant Secretary to the Board of Revenue, to whom we have since been indebted for many more, and more important favours, introduced to me a native pressman named Chand.* This man had left a situation not long before, and was about to go to Calcutta for employment; but, having married at Allahabad, was willing to remain there. I agreed with him to serve me for stipulated wages, and to put him upon half pay till our printing-house should be opened. This was the commencement of gathering an establishment about myself, that afterwards grew to something much larger and more important. This man continued in the press till I left it, and was still with Mr. Hay when I passed the place on my return to America.

The next step was the taking of an apprentice. Any person who may have seen the little book, published by the Board of Publication, called "Poor Blind Sally," will be interested by the fact that my apprentice was her brother John, and will be glad to

* *The moon.* The name of this luminary is masculine in Hindustání.

hear that he was foreman of the establishment under
Mr. Hay, when I last saw it. John and his sister had
been separated from their mother, and left entirely
destitute, by the most distressing circumstances, and
had been brought up in our orphan asylums. We
took John into our house, and made preparations for
a very small beginning of a printing-house.

By recurring to the description of our bungalow,
in the second chapter, it will be seen that we had
bathing-rooms at three corners. In one of these we
opened the English type and put it in cases. John
had never seen a type before, and of course nearly
all the work had to be done by my own hands. We
set up a stand, and John commenced his work, in the
bathing-room, on a little catechism by John Brown
of Haddington. The press was set up in one of the
out-houses near the kitchen. A man, named Dillá,
was hired to assist Chand. He was quite unacquainted
with the business. Thus was commenced *The Presbyterian Mission Press** at Allahabad. We could
not expect to get on very fast when, with the exception of an imperfectly instructed pressman, everything
was to be formed by my own exertions. It was a
small beginning; but it grew, as will be seen in the
sequel, till it sent forth the gospel to the farthest
corners of that part of India.

In a short time after this, a Persian character compositor offered his services. He had been a Musalmán,
but now professed to be a Christian; and he was, indeed, a member of the Baptist Church at Cawnpore,
having been baptized by a Mr. Greenway. His name
was Husain Bakhsh. He was a sharp and active
fellow, with sufficient learning for the post for which

* This was the *name* of the Press, by which it was known to
Government as registered. We wished the name to suggest principles. I was once or twice amused by noticing the repugnance of a
good friend to this name. He was an Episcopal Chaplain, who
was having some work done. Still he was not violent.

5*

he offered himself, but not very well taught as a printer. He would have done us good service, however, had he not been a drunkard, quarrelsome, and dishonest. Under his instructions we made up cases for the Persian type. Let printers imagine my disgust and dismay, when it was found that, instead of the one pair of cases, which each man has before him, in setting up English type, we had to put up two pairs, end to end, and also another case at each end, crosswise, on wings, in order to place all the sorts. We went on trying the type, and soon discovered that several necessary combinations of letters were impossible with our single letters, and that there were no compounds for them in the fount, although we had already a most discouraging number of compounds: many could be made no otherwise than by the knife and file. We cut, and filed, and stuffed paper into the vacant places made by filing away a part of the bodies of some of the letters, and resorted to many other means of making the letters join properly. A job had been offered to us which was profitable, and which I was exceedingly anxious to do, and to do well, as it was the first.

Let me here gratefully record, that the first patron of the press was E. A. Reade, Esq., then collector and magistrate of Goruckpore, and who was still in India when I left, a member of the Board of Revenue at Agra. He gave us the printing of what were called *Dastaks*, which are a kind of summons to be served on those who are in arrears as to land revenue. The prices then paid by the Government for public printing were such, that it was well worth while to take pains to secure it. The dastaks contained a little table work, for which we had no rules. Our only resource was either tin cut out with shears, or sheet copper wrought by a common blacksmith. The compositor was not competent to do anything that required recourse to expedients; and my acquaintance with the language was as yet so imperfect, that it was with great difficulty that I understood what was required, or made myself understood.

The cases were set up in the back verandah of the bungalow, and my attention was divided between John in the bathing-room, Chand in the outhouse, Husain Bakhsh in the verandah, and a sick wife in the house. But after several days' effort and experimenting, we were successful; the dastaks were pronounced passable, and were printed. The labour and anxiety which I underwent in this thing were great, but the success was proportionately pleasant; and, beside this, we learned what were the chief deficiencies of our type, and were enabled to send to Serampore for the sorts most necessary. About the same time we discovered that one of the founts of English type brought from America was imperfect, not having a single *b* or *c* in it. We got these made at Calcutta; but they never stood very well with the other letters.

After a few months the compositor, Husain Bakhsh, got drunk, quarrelled with another native Christian, accused him of stealing a shawl from him, and made such a tumult, that we were obliged to part with him at once. I have never heard of him since. Here it may be said, that some of our greatest troubles have arisen from unprincipled Musalmáns, who professed to become Christians, when they had no religious convictions whatever. They are forbidden by the Qurán to drink anything that intoxicates; and, though they would have no conscience about it, yet the Musalmán community would expel them for notorious indulgence. For this reason we have found that some of them have professed Christianity, supposing that they might then drink without reproach or danger. Occasionally we have learned, that the hope of an increased income has also induced men of this sort to join us. Generally these things are discovered before a man can make a profession of our religion; for missionaries are usually very cautious. But sometimes they have been deceived. Chaplains, some of whom are mere formalists, have baptized men that have been nothing but a grief and scandal ever afterward. The following is one instance.

We had a man in our employment, in the press, for some time as an inquirer. He had a wife, not originally a Musalmán, but of a very low caste of Hindús, who had become a Musalmán in order to marry him. They had three or four children. The man urged me to baptize them all, which could not be done, as he gave very little satisfaction by his progress in Christian knowledge, or by his conduct. He met with an accident while drawing water from a well, by which his cheek bone was fractured; and he was laid up for three months, before the ugly wound could be fully cured, and then it left a bad scar. I paid his wages all this time, as if he had been at work, and procured him the best of medical attendance. After he got well, and urged me more and more to baptize him, I told him that it could not be done at present; that he did not seem to me like a man on whom had passed any spiritual change. On this he said he would leave me, and go to Lucknow, his native place. He was accordingly paid up, and we parted amicably. On his way to Lucknow, he called on my friend, the Rev. W. H. Perkins,* at Cawnpore, and wished to be baptized by him. This was declined, for the same reasons that had made me refuse. While with Mr. Perkins, he was talking about me, and hinting that I was no better than I should be; when Mr. Perkins asked him what he meant. He answered that I was a most gross and violent oppressor; and that, if anything went wrong in the printing-house, I made nothing of throwing the mallet at any one's head, or striking him with anything that came to hand; and added: "Look here, sir," laying his finger on the scar on his cheek bone.

* Now of Hampstead, near London.

"Did he do that?" asked Mr. Perkins. The man nodded, and said, "And for no fault too." Mr. Perkins at once doubted, and dismissed him; and afterwards took measures to ascertain whether there was any truth in the story. Both he and I, though by that time by no means inexperienced men, were rather astonished at the magnitude, malignity, and causelessness of the fabrication. This man and his family were shortly afterwards baptized by a Chaplain at Lucknow, and, as I was told, while displaying no more of the spirit of Christ than before.

Another anecdote, relating to our troubles from unprincipled Mohammedans, will be found in the fourth chapter.

Dillú, the assistant pressman, was an example of making a profession of Christianity for gain. He was a Musalmán, and lived with a Musalmán bad woman, to whom he had never been married. They professed to be penitent and asked to be baptized. Though this request was not granted, they were married in Christian fashion, by the Rev. James Wilson, before my arrival at Allahabad. After long trial the wife was proved to be no better than before, and Dillú was convicted of stealing paper from the printing-house, and sent to jail. They, not having been baptized, fell back into the ordinary Musalmán community, but not before they had done us a damage by being connected with us.

There was a singular case connected with this business of Dillú's. The paper, which he stole from the press, he sold to three or four persons. He was convicted, and sent to jail for three months. One of the receivers was also sentenced to one month's imprisonment. Another, when he heard of the search that was being made for the paper, undertook to burn that which he had—about five quires. Two of my servants, the house-bearer and the printing-house watchman, who were on the look-out for this man, caught him burning the paper, and snatched it away from the fire when only a corner had been burned. They brought it to me at once. I examined it, and knew it to be some of the stolen paper, because it was American, and there was no more like it in that region. It was night when it was brought; and as nothing could be done about it before the next day, we placed it in one of the common rooms of the house, intending to proceed in the business in the morning. But when the paper was examined in the morning, it was evidently not the same—some native paper had been burned in a similar manner, and substituted for it. Of course the receiving of stolen goods could not now be proved. The man had, during the night, bribed my servants to allow the exchange, so that he might escape. On questioning the servants about it, they, of course, denied all knowledge of the exchange. One of them boldly declared that there had been no exchange at all. The other, when asked, replied in the indirect and twisting style of true Hindustání cunning, "My lord, what can I say?" A hundred times I varied and repeated the question; and as many times he managed to give an indirect or evasive answer. He had baffled me so long, that it became to me a singular trial of skill between us, and I was determined to have a direct answer; but "How should the slave know anything about it?"—"That was damaged by fire, and this is damaged by fire; and does not that indicate they are the same?" These and similar replies were all I could get. At last I put the question, "Do you think the paper has been changed?" and demanded that his answer should be a simple and unqualified yes, or no. I explained to him, and threatened him with instant dismissal; and at last, when under the influence of the most abject fear, with the greatest reluctance he whispered *No*. Now this was the answer he meant to give all the time. It was not fear of lying that made him evade a direct reply;

but it was the cunning, equivocating spirit, which is
ingrained in almost all that people, that cannot make
up its mind to walk straight forward in either right
or wrong.

It was necessary to build a printing-house, and we
had not money sufficient to do it at once, as it ought
to have been done; but we did the best thing that
our circumstances allowed. We put up clay walls,
and made floors as described in the second chapter,
where bungalows are spoken of. The roof was intended to be more safe as to fire, and more durable,
than a thatch, and was made of tiles. These tiles I
was advised to join with lime, and did so at considerable expense; but the first rainy season brought all
the lime to the ground. At first only two large
rooms were built, and a small store-room for paper.
Afterward two more rooms were added—one for the
oriental type, and one for miscellaneous purposes.
The floors of these rooms were soon broken up by the
constant trampling upon them; types dropped upon
the ground were commonly lost; and various other
reasons combined to cause us to make the floors over
again, using flag-stones. Our windows were only
venetians, and did not keep dust from the cases. But
this was the best that we could do with the means at
command.

To explain some of my mishaps, it is necessary to
tell how lime is made in that part of India; and this
will not be uninteresting to those who are accustomed
to that which is so entirely different. Some lime is
made from stone dug out of quarries, and burned in
the same manner as in America; but this is very expensive, and is used only for whitewash, or the finest
parts of work. The lime for common use is altogether different. It is made from *kankar*. This is a
kind of limestone found in clay strata (I will leave
scientific men to say how) in irregular nodules, rough
and jagged, much like some specimens of what is

called bog iron ore. This is collected, and a kiln made of it in the following manner. First a layer of cow-dung, which has been kneaded and made into flat cakes and dried (called *kauda*), is placed on the ground in a circle. Then a layer of the kankar is placed upon it; then another layer of the kauda, and another of the kankar; and so on, each layer being a little contracted, till a mound of five feet in height is raised. This is then set on fire, and the burning of the kauda bakes the kankar sufficiently to make the greater part of it slake. There are several modes of cheating in this business. First, the man who sells the kauda may cheat, by mixing clay or ashes with it when it is made. The clay, of course, adulterates the lime; for the kankar is so small that the whole mass, ashes and all, must pass for lime—there is no separating them. Secondly, the kankar, being dug out of clay, may be allowed to have a great deal adhere to it, which ought to be shaken off; and even lumps of clay may be put in on purpose. Thirdly, after the lime is burnt, and perhaps sold by specimen, ashes and clay are mixed with it. As this lime always has a dirty colour, it requires a good deal of experience, and a practical knowledge of the tests applied to it, to detect these adulterations. I had unsuspiciously bought lime that was chiefly clay and ashes, and therefore the cement of my roof became mud, and the floors soon became dust.

I have said that there was one room in the printing house for miscellaneous purposes. The press for smoothing printed sheets was in this room. This reminds me, that at first we had no such press, and used a washerwoman's smoothing iron when sheets *must* be smoothed. Various other odd jobs of work were done in this room. But one of the main purposes that it served was that of church, or chapel. In it we held the Hindustání worship on the Sabbath for a long time. It was not convenient; and the

appearance of worldly business, presented by the
standing press and piles of paper, was unfavourable
to the feeling of sacredness, that ought to be assisted
by all circumstances in our public worship. At
length it became too small for the congregation, and
we were compelled to provide another place, which
will hereafter be described.

At an early period we built a depository for the
tracts and portions of the Scriptures that we printed.
It was a small room of about twenty feet square, and
attached to the bungalow. After about two years
this was found to be too small, and was taken away.
When it was built, none of us had any notion that it
would ever prove too small. Such are the disadvan-
tages of having to feel one's way in everything.
Instead of it, we then put up a long building on the
north side of the yard, near the house. This contained a small room at one end for the safe keeping
of the mission tents and other apparatus used in
itinerating. Next to this was a room of about forty
feet by twenty, which was the proper tract and book
depository. At the other end was another small
room, in which the bound books of the British and
Foreign Bible Society, and of the American Tract
Society, were kept for sale. In this room we had our
morning family worship in Hindustání. The greater
part of the native Christians attended this exercise,
and our heathen and Mohammedan servants also,
whenever they could be induced to do so by anything
short of compulsion, which we thought it not right to
use. The walls of this building were of burnt bricks
laid up with lime. Experience had taught me how
to buy lime; and this wall is not likely to break from
the weakness of its materials. The back wall has no
windows except narrow ones close to the roof for
ventilation. Each room has a large door in front,
and there are glass windows between them. The
front and one end are protected by a verandah, cov-

ered with tiles, and supported by slender octagonal stone pillars. The bricks are painted red, and the lime between them white, so that the appearance is very neat. The roof is flat. It is made by first laying beams across at short intervals, then covering them with flagstones, and over them making a covering in much the same way as floors are made as described in the second chapter.

The depository, and the new printing-house which will be mentioned below, were built in this manner, because of two great dangers to which books, or anything perishable, are exposed when they are to be stored throughout the year. The first of these dangers is leakage. A more perishable roof might let through a stream of water, which would do great damage. Beside this, it requires such constant repairs that it is not so cheap in the end as one that costs a greater original outlay.

The greater danger, however, is from the white ant. This little insect is one of the greatest plagues of India. It is somewhat larger than the small black ant in America, but nearer the size of that than of the larger. It is soft and *watery*—a finger placed upon it crushes it with the greatest ease without rubbing it at all; and yet, weak and delicate as it is, it bores through or consumes everything softer than a stone; destroys immense beams in the roofs of houses; strips the dry and corrugated bark off the largest trees; comes up through hard lime floors and attacks whatever is placed upon them; enters a box, and perhaps in a single night, leaves you nothing but tatters and a quantity of clay; bores through the foot of a bookcase, and eats *to the quick* a whole shelf full of books in a few hours. They always live in the ground; and some experiments, which I made upon them, convinced me that if their communication with the ground be interrupted, they will cease their work, and scatter away, unless they can re-establish a similar road to head-quarters. The reason of this is, that they always cover themselves, whenever they emerge from the ground, with wet clay, which soon becomes dry, and possesses considerable tenacity. They make with this an arched passage, wide enough to pass each other in it, wherever they go; and whenever they reach an article they intend to eat, they cover it over with a sheet of this clay, under which are numerous arches of this kind. In these they use their terrible mandibles with incredible speed and dexterity, filling up with the clay any space they may thus make vacant. In this way it often happens that a painted beam of timber, the outside of which they will not eat because of the poisonous quality of the paint, and which therefore externally appears to be sound, is found to be a mass of clay held together by the tougher bits of wood, that the little devourers either did not choose to try their teeth on, or left to brace their work. They make their way up through the walls of a bungalow to the height of thirty feet, and eat the grass of the thatch, filling up the space left with their honeycombed masses of clay, to be brought down into the rooms in streams of mud by the first heavy rain that falls, unless previously discovered and removed. Any article left carelessly on the ground over night is very likely to be taken up riddled in the morning. A straw, left on the ground in this manner, will be pretty sure to be replaced, before the next day, by a line of clay, forming a covered path. From all I can learn of them they do not seem to be of the same species with the African white ant—at least they do not build ant-hills like them.* A friend once told me that they were the same, and built their houses above ground when climate, water, and other circumstances were different from those of the plains of India; and that he had seen these ant-hills in the

---

* One of Parley's works falls into the error here alluded to.

tract of country lying along the foot of the Himmá-láyá mountains. But when I recently rode through a part of that same tract, I satisfied myself that this was a mistake. I saw what I at first took to be their hills. They stood up four or five feet high here and there in the forest; the rain had guttered many of them into various angles, and left pinnacles standing up, so that often they presented no bad model for the exterior of a Gothic castle or church. But when I examined them, hoping to see the interior arrange-ments of a tribe, they proved to be but the ordinary work of the insects over a stump, which they had de-voured. For, when a forest tree is cut down, they leave the stump till it is at least partially dead, and then build over and eat it. It is supposed that the instinct of covering their work with clay is given to them to protect themselves from being destroyed by birds. To preserve our books and paper from being destroyed by these insects, it was necessary to make the buildings as perfect as possible, and to resort to various plans to keep the insects at a distance. If sheet-iron be placed under the feet of a book-shelf, they will build across it, and climb the leg. We have to apply tar, or set the feet into vessels of oil. The shelves must be placed at a distance from the wall, or the ants will reach them by building out pipes of clay from the wall. These pipes are sometimes found as much as eight or nine inches long.

From time to time additions were made to the establishment, both of men and apparatus. A Per-sian compositor, and one for the Nágarí, were got up from Calcutta. A second and larger fount of Nágarí type was procured, as well as a small fount of Arabic, with vowel-points. After a time, as our business increased, a new fount of type did not cause such a sen-sation as to be noticed particularly. We were pre-pared for, and performed, printing in Arabic, San-scrit, Urdú, Hindí—the two last in two characters each—and in English. We bought a small fount of Greek, and made one of Hebrew, and executed a work containing a great deal of both.

The first tract printed in the Arabic letter was in the Urdú dialect, entitled "A'quibat kí bábat"—On the Future State. The first in the Nágarí letter was in the Hindí dialect, called "Nicodemus, or The Inquirer." Both these were written by the Rev. James Wilson, then senior missionary at Allahabad. The first thing printed in the Urdú-Roman was a translation, by Mr. Wilson, of Gallaudet's "Child's Book on the Soul." Thus Mr. Wilson had the honour and privilege of giving their first employment to three parts of our apparatus.

The constant breaking of the Persian type and the Nágarí vowel-points, and various deficiencies which were continually coming to view, kept us sending to Calcutta for sorts. My patience was nearly worn out; and John C. Marshman, Esq., of Serampore, at length advised me to have a punch-cutter and type-caster of my own, saying that from long experience he was quite convinced we could never carry on our work in the oriental alphabets without one, at such a distance from a type-foundry. Allahabad is five hundred miles distant from Calcutta by land; and in those days a steamer took nearly a month to get up the stream. This caused delays that were disastrous, and induced me to engage a man through Mr. Marshman, and to get moulds and other apparatus for casting type on a small scale. This foundry turned out for us, from time to time, all the oriental type which we required. It made a fount of Arabic type of a size a little larger than that which we had before; a large quantity of Nágarí, on which, before I left the place, we had printed nearly half of a new Hindí translation of the Bible, chiefly made by Mr. Owen of our Mission, and the printing of which was left for Mr. Hay to complete; a larger size of the same letter

6*

for head-lines, &c.; a fount of Hebrew, for a work on Scripture proper names, intended to aid translators in securing uniformity of spelling; and many other things. Two young men, who had been in the Asylum, were taught to cast, and employed in this work after they were married. The Hindú man, whom we procured from Calcutta, would not teach these boys to cut punches. He used to make a great mystery of this part of his business, utterly refusing to be seen at his work. In order to bring him to compliance, I hired a Bangálí itinerant engraver who came along, and set him to cutting punches. He had never tried it before, but soon succeeded very well; and under his instructions Joseph, one of the above young men, went to work. When the regular man saw that we should succeed in getting punches without his aid, and that we should soon be able to part with him, he listened to my threats of dismissal, and consented to teach Joseph. We were pretty well under weigh, in this respect, when I left Allahabad; and on passing it again in 1853 I found that Mr. Hay had carried on my scheme, and that Joseph had acquired a good degree of skill, and learned a trade that makes him a most useful man.

The printing-house gradually grew, the workmen improved, and the means of doing all that was desirable were constantly accumulated, till my separation from it. The work done at it was superior to that of other presses above Calcutta, until other establishments were induced to adopt improvements. The press gathered about itself a congregation of more than forty native Christians, some of them converts, and some from orphan asylums. Constant efforts were made to work in all the Christians who could be procured, that were at all fit for the employments offered, in place of the heathen and Musalmáns, who were necessarily employed at first. It afforded facilities for employing inquirers. But its direct usefulness, in furnishing tracts and Scriptures for distribution throughout the country, is what is mainly to be looked at. It has printed works for this purpose to the average amount of fully three millions of duodecimo pages annually. A large portion of this work has been of the nature of tracts to set forth Christian truth, or to show the untruth of heathenism. We published several editions of each of the single Gospels, of the four Gospels and Acts bound together, of Luke and Acts, of some of the epistles, of the Psalms, Proverbs, and of Genesis and first twenty chapters of Exodus. For a more particular account of our labours in preparing and publishing works of various kinds, see the seventh chapter. These tracts and books are scattered amongst all missions, whether of our own Board or of other societies, from Dinapore and Tirhoot to the Panjáb. They have been distributed in journeys, at fairs, and at the mission stations, till they have been carried all over Upper India, and the effect of them has been felt in some of the most secluded villages in the remotest corners of the land.

The press has also caused the writing of books by affording facilities for publication. It is with the surest conviction of its truth that I say, that many of our most valuable treatises would not have been written or translated, had not this press been in existence. When we come to the chapter on preaching, it will be seen that the missionaries have much time when the climate does not allow them to be out of doors, even if they had strength enough to be engaged in preaching all day; and that the nature of a great deal of our preaching is such that it affords us leisure for the composition or translation of books. Therefore any instrumentality that brings this part of their time into profitable use is most valuable. This the mission press did to a great extent.

We had at Allahabad an orphan asylum, which

has already been incidentally mentioned. It was formed at first principally from children, whose parents perished in the great famine of 1837—8. This famine prevailed over the region on both sides of the Jumna river, from above Allahabad to the region of Delhi, causing a terrible destruction of life. The Government and private individuals did all that was possible to alleviate its horrors; and, amongst other benevolent efforts, much was done to collect and feed children whose parents had died or deserted them. Many of these children were afterwards reclaimed by relatives; and hundreds more were handed over to various orphan asylums, that were formed in connection with various missions. A large asylum was formed for girls at Cawnpore, under the Mission of the Society for the Propagation of the Gospel in foreign parts. A large one for boys was formed under the Church Mission at Benares. Our own, for both boys and girls, were formed at Futteh-gurh and Allahabad. There was another large asylum for both sexes at Agra; beside some minor ones at different places. Had it been possible to preserve the lives of even half of these unfortunate children after receiving them into the asylums, it would have caused us to have now much larger nominal Christian communities; but they came so debilitated and diseased that the greater part died, although attended to most kindly and assiduously. It was a most melancholy spectacle. The greater part of some parties of them died in a very short time, and of the remainder the majority did not survive to reach mature age. The number of people that died of starvation and famine-fever during the prevalence of the scarcity, great as it was, probably did not nearly equal those who died slowly afterward in consequence of disease and debility contracted then.

The female part of the asylum at Allahabad was then under the care of Mrs. Wilson; and after our arrival Mr. Morrison made over the boys to Mr. Freeman. The boys were all being taught the elements of a plain education in their own language; and it was intended to bring up the promising ones for teachers. Some of the boys were dull, and not capable of being easily fitted for any literary employment; and it was highly desirable that they should be taught some manual occupation, by which to support themselves. At the same time many of them were so young, that, to have taken them at once to the press, would have made it necessary to set up something like another orphan asylum for them there. For these reasons it was thought best to have the book-binders work under Mr. Freeman's charge, and the boys do all the folding and sewing. This plan was adhered to till nearly all the boys, who were employed in this part of the work, were married and left the asylum, and Mr. Freeman himself left the country to visit America, when the bindery was removed to the press. We had sometimes one, and sometimes another native as head binder; but no one was satisfactory. They work, as I have already said carpenters do, always sitting on the ground; and all their processes are most clumsy and slow. The results, also, are far from satisfactory. We made up apparatus like that used in Europe and America, and strove manfully against their prejudices and habits. Yet the *vis inertiae* of such workmen is such as people in America cannot conceive of. They never attempted an improvement that was suggested to them till they were forced to it; and never were forced to anything of this kind without spoiling more or less work or material. Their wages were not great. We paid the best Hindú binder we ever had only seven dollars a month; but the work they turned out was dearer than that done in New York by men who made two dollars a day. Had it been practicable, it would have been cheaper to send our binding to New York to be done. This part of our establishment I could not bring into a satisfactory condition; but I left it to Mr. Hay with a Christian foreman, and several Christian workmen, who were improving.

Amongst the last things that were done under my superintendence of the printing establishment was the building of a new house for it. The perishable character of the original structure has been spoken of before. The new one is built in the same substantial manner with the depository before spoken of. It has a large press-room, with a store-room for paper attached to it; a larger room for compositors; and a fine bindery. There is also a small room for an office for proof-readers, and many other conveniences. The foundry is in a room in a corner tower, so isolated by thick walls that danger from fire is avoided. This was built without exceeding the allowances for the press; and we were enabled to do so by taking in job-work.

The practice of doing job-work was necessary for another reason. Having to keep men for printing several different characters, our allowances would not keep us at work all the time, and it was necessary to have other work to employ the people a part of the time; because they must be paid regularly, or they could not be retained. It is true that this arrangement causes the superintendent a great deal of merely secular work. Very little help could be obtained from the people on the establishment as to proof-reading, except in the native dialects—and even in these their want of accuracy was often visible. Their education in English was so defective that they could never be trusted for a single word. The compositors would read manuscript, if quite plain; but if not so, they would put together whatever they thought the letters looked like, often making the most impossible combinations of letters, both amusing and provoking, which they did not suspect to be other than good English words. Mrs. Warren was my assistant in proof-reading; and I should often have been overwhelmed with business had it not been for her help. It often happened to me, that correspondence on business, the superintendence and proof-reading of job-work, and business connected with the treasurership of the mission, took up two-thirds of my time. For this reason there ought to be a lay superintendent of the printing establishment, if the proper person could be procured. He might have charge of the secular business of the mission generally, and be immensely useful. But, though the press did hinder other things that might have been done, I neither repent nor regret my connection with it; it has been so useful an agent in our work that it would be wrong to be sorry for having been employed in it. Had I not had charge of it, probably I might had more to do with Sanscrit and philosophy, and been more useful than I have been in some of the higher branches of missionary labour, that would both have been more pleasant, and more esteemed by the public. But such a sacrifice, if such there has been, ought to be lightly regarded. He who has been furnished with a useful field of labour by the Lord of the harvest, and allowed to occupy it so long, has every reason to be thankful.

The question may be raised, how long will it be necessary to carry on such establishments as mission presses? The answer must be, till some of the native Christians can take them off our hands. They are necessary now for various reasons, especially as affording employment to the native Christians. But if any of our Christians should prove to be such business men that they can take the presses over, and gradually pay for them, doing our work and employing our people, it would be better to transfer them, and so gradually to disconnect the missions from secular business. This, however, may not be practicable for several years to come.

CHAPTER IV.

CATECHISTS: THEIR TRAINING, CHARACTER AND USEFULNESS.

As the plan of this work is not so much to give an account of my own labours, as to take occasion from them to give information as to the working of our mission, and the character of the people, the subject above named is brought in, although I have had no more than an ordinary share in this part of our work.

It is unnecessary to take much pains to explain at length the importance of having native helpers in a mission, because this is generally pretty well understood. It is easy to perceive how they may be made most efficient agents amongst the people of their own countries; and how important their office is as a step towards a native ministry. Our mission at Allahabad made early efforts to secure the services of such helpers. Our choice, however, was confined to few men, and it was hard to find native Christians who were well educated, fluent, and of satisfactory character. Although we have helpers there, who are such indeed, and a comfort and joy to us, yet some of our main trials were connected with the training and employment of this class of men. And as this book is written to gratify the reasonable curiosity of the Church, and to lead her members to sympathize with, and pray for, their agents in foreign lands, it will be the object of this chapter to show what a catechist is intended to be and to do, and what are some of our experiences connected with them.

Generally each mission, and frequently each missionary, trains his catechists as he may be able, without following any plan laid down by the whole body; in fact, each does the best he can, according to his circumstances. In the beginning this was the way in which we were obliged to go on. Every missionary needed somebody to aid him in reading in the streets, and in the work of distributing tracts. In the hot and dusty towns and villages of India very few men can speak in the open air, in the midst of various noises, more than half an hour at a time—few even so long. Yet it is often desirable to hold a crowd of people longer. In this way it becomes necessary to have a native reader, who can read aloud the tract or portion of Scripture that is to be talked of, and can also speak under the care of the missionary. And when the talk is over, and tracts are offered to those who can read, he can afford great assistance in examining applicants. For these purposes men were so necessary that many missionaries were compelled to accept the services of those who would have been deemed unfit for such an employment where a greater field of choice existed. In this way it happened that all degrees of catechists were employed: boys from school, who were only allowed to read to the people; some, a little more advanced, who could parrot a few trains of Christian argument and exhortation, which they had been taught; and some, who had an education, and could talk and argue, from the stores of their own minds, with more or less ability.

Our missionaries felt this state of things to be undesirable; and at the meeting of our Synod at Agra, in 1848, on the second day of the session it was

Resolved, That a Committee be appointed to report a scheme for regulating the qualifications and licensure of catechists; and that Messrs. Warren and Janvier be the said Committee.

7

At a subsequent session this Committee reported a scheme, a part of which is as follows:

The Committee appointed to report a scheme for regulating the qualifications and licensure of catechists, reported. The report was accepted, and with a few amendments was adopted, and is as follows:

1. That in the opinion of your Committee a greater degree of uniformity in the qualifications of catechists is highly desirable; and as we suppose, a feeling of this kind extensively prevails, and on it the action is grounded, which has brought the subject before Synod:

2. Your Committee would therefore recommend that the following attainments in learning be required of those who shall hereafter seek the office of catechist:

(1.) The ability to compose with facility and general correctness in one of the native languages or dialects—that is, the Urdú, Hindí, or Panjábí, writing it in the native character.

(2.) A full understanding of, and capability of using, the Romanizing system now prevalent in our missions.

(3.) The knowledge of an outline of Scripture History.

(4.) The difference between the Mosaic and Christian dispensations.

(5.) The knowledge of an outline of Church History.

(6.) The same of Didactic Theology.

(7.) The same of General History, Ancient and Modern.

(8.) The same of the principles of Interpretation.

(9.) And that the Presbytery should strongly recommend to every candidate the acquisition of the Persian or Sanscrit language.

The scheme thus adopted by the Synod also provided for the oversight of candidates, their examination, and their licensure by Presbytery. This was a very fair beginning; but it is to be feared that the same causes that kept catechists from being properly trained and tried before, still operate to some extent; and that the Presbyteries have not yet been brought to take this matter up with that perseverance which alone can bring about a proper state of things. One reason of this is, that our Synod has failed to meet according to its adjournment. Distance, expense, and the inconvenience of leaving our stations, when there are so few to carry on so many ordinary operations, are the usual reasons given for not having a meeting of Synod; and at particular times there may be private reasons, affecting individuals, equally operative. But notwithstanding these reasons the Synod ought to have met, and seen that the scheme as to catechists, was carried out as well as some other things that required attention. It is no discredit to us as individuals to say, that we needed the influence of Synodical control. Present convenience is always operating to make us postpone and modify some things; and men will not act in accordance with a system, without control, as steadily as they would under its influence. If they would so act, then Synods could be everywhere dispensed with. If it were determined that Synods should meet, and each Presbytery were instructed to arrange matters so that some of its members should attend, and unite this object with a preaching tour, all that is necessary might easily be done. The home duties of absentees could be temporarily discharged by their brethren, and a part of our office (that of Evangelists) might be in more active use.

It is certain, however, that something has been done towards carrying out this scheme; and the catechists, no doubt, will improve year by year. If some central institution could be established, in which all the candidates for this office could be gathered, and taught together, according to a scheme approved by the Synod, the much desired object of a higher and more uniform education would be secured. If at Agra, which is nearly central to our stations, there were always three or four picked men fixed, they could take charge of this institution in addition to their other duties. This would be the completion of the general scheme, of which our high-schools at Agra are a part. There might be two departments in the school—one for candidates for the ministry, and one for mere catechists. It is probable that the high-school at Agra may produce some candidates for the higher department, as well as the native churches. The catechists would be much more likely to be regularly taught in such an institution, than they are at present, and could be practised, as they are now, in labouring with the missionaries. This would save a great deal of labour. Many missionaries are now employed in giving desultory and perfunctory instructions. The teachers of a theological school could both relieve them, and teach more systematically. At present, also, every man uses such books as he can procure, and of proper ones there is a great lack. While we have no central institution, individuals will have different opinions about what books should be prepared; and without union nothing will be done. But the central institution would lead to efforts to supply this lack, which would, doubtless, be successful, and give as much satisfaction to all as the nature of the case admits.

On the other hand it may be said, that there are many reasons for training catechists at their several stations. In this way more may be raised up. If all were to be at the expense of sending their candidates to the seminary, and supporting them there, it may be supposed that fewer would be taken up. Each candidate might also receive more personal attention, and be more employed in preaching, if each were under the care of a separate station; though the many engagements of the missionaries would render the personal attention somewhat doubtful. There is no doubt that a seminary could not combine all its own advantages with those of more private training: a comparison of the two modes should be made; and that chosen which offered the greatest facilities for accomplishing the end. And it would not be necessary to send every candidate to the institution—some latitude might be allowed to the Presbyteries in this respect.

When the catechists, as a class, become well educated and gentlemanly men, and exert an influence on native society, visiting and being visited by their Hindú and Musalmán neighbours, we may expect them to be very useful—perhaps as much so as European or American missionaries. We have seen something of this; many native gentlemen now visit them, and prejudice against them is wearing away. At first they were, of course, regarded as renegades, and often they have been called on to endure cruel contumely and scorn; to be the subject of wicked slanders and reproaches; and to be persecuted to any degree that was in the power of men who had not law on their side. A catechist, labouring with me, has been assailed in my presence with charges of having forsaken his ancestral faith for the sake of high pay and sensual allurements. This catechist was working for eight dollars a month, supporting a wife and two children on his pay, and living in such a manner that all his life and arrangements could be easily seen; and his assailant called him a mercenary dog, and said that it was publicly known that he had thirty-five dollars a month, and a woman in addition to his wife. The man bore this abuse very well. The only sign of impatience which he displayed was to answer, "You Musalmáns are accustomed to make converts by such means; so it is not much to be wondered at if you suppose Christians make them in the same manner." His counter accusation was so true that nothing more could be said. I added an invitation to the slanderer to come and see our place, and examine into all our affairs. Lately the natives have slowly come to perceive that there may be such a thing as a native having a sincere conviction of the truth of Christianity; and they generally treat the catechists with great consideration.

It has already been said that a catechist is employed to assist the missionary to read and distri-

7*

bute tracts and Scriptures, and to speak when he
can. His duty also is, when his qualifications are
above the lowest order, to go out by himself when
the missionary cannot go. As I was employed
about the press I could not go out every day. I
very much wished to do so; but other duties often
made it impossible. I therefore made constant efforts
to keep my native assistant going without me. But
this is very discouraging work for a native man.
They are neither so successful in obtaining hearers,
nor so respectfully treated when alone as when a
European is with them. My first catechist was not
very fluent, and of no very commanding aspect; and
thus was not so well listened to as to make his work
attractive. It was with some difficulty, for these reasons, that he could be induced to work alone. Still
a great deal is done by the catechists in this way.
They may not be able to gather a crowd around
them, as the white man almost always can; but they
get into conversation with a few. They may often
sit down with some of the people, and discuss some
point of truth. If they can do nothing more, they will
keep in circulation the *bruit* of a religion offered to
the people's acceptance. It is also usually their duty
to visit the vernacular schools, and give the boys
instruction in the Catechism, and exhort all who may
be around, and aid the missionary in his work of teaching religious truths to these schools, which he also
visits. Another of their duties is to assist the missionaries at the *melas*, or fairs. Still another is to
accompany the missionaries on their preaching tours.
If he be a man of sufficient learning, he may act as the
missionary's assistant in literary matters. Bábú John
Harí and Munshí Mirza John Bez, catechists at Allahabad, were of great use to me in my literary labours.
They assisted me to revise a translation of the Confession of Faith and both Catechisms of our Church,
in Urdú. The translation was made by the Rev.

James Wilson, and would not have needed much revision had it not been made on the principle of a *free*, rather than a *close*, rendering of the original. It was determined to bring it closer to the original, and at the same time to preserve the Urdú idiom. Any one who has been engaged in translation, knows the difficulty of such a work. These two men were long engaged in it with me. We often used to labour one, and sometimes several hours over a single sentence. Mirza, who is something of a poet, used to turn my prose translation of poetry into Urdú verse, in such works as the Urdú translation of the Dairyman's Daughter and the Young Cottager. Harí has translated the Indian Pilgrim and Pilgrim's Progress into Urdú. His knowledge of English is sufficient to do so, except that he occasionally requires assistance in a single sentence.

We have long felt that when we should have a sufficient number of faithful catechists, we ought to plant them in the larger towns around our mission stations. At Allahabad we often talked of several towns, at distances of ten to twenty miles from the station, at which it would be desirable to place catechists, to act both as schoolmasters and preachers. Another part of the plan would have been, to have one of the missionaries frequently visit these places. This was not carried out, because we all thought that we had no men, who could be spared from the station, that were fitted to work out such a scheme. After my departure from that place it was tried by Mr. Owen; but his agent proved not to have the necessary stamina and skill. Some later attempts of this kind have been made, which seem to be more successful; and when our native assistants become accustomed to the idea of personal responsibility, these attempts will be still more successful. We must take the risk of failures, or keep our helpers under such surveillance that they will fail to acquire independence and strength of character, or a spirit of enterprise. Without doubt we must prepare for, and execute some such scheme as this, if we would thoroughly preach the gospel through our districts. Missionaries should be set apart to the superintendence of such circles of catechists, and the means should be provided of travelling amongst them all the time when the weather permits, and of making flying visits to them throughout the hot season.

After these general remarks, the reader may like to see some facts, connected with the catechists, intended to illustrate our joys and our sorrows that arise from this source. Some of our native helpers read English. This fact will show the propriety of my generally concealing names; though to do so will render the anecdotes less piquant.

Shortly after my settlement at Allahabad, we received a convert from a high caste of Hindús. He could read very well; and after a short course of instruction, was set at work under the care of the Rev. J. Wilson. He learned readily, and spoke fluently; and I have seen very few men who appeared more zealous, or more willing to work in the sphere appointed for them. At the great fair at Allahabad, I have often admired the patience with which he bore contradiction, the mildness with which he answered objections, and the versatility of talent by which he adapted his subjects and manner to the ever varying circumstances around him. On one occasion, for example, he was holding an argument with a Bráhman, involving some points of their philosophy, when the Bráhman suddenly uttered some sharp sarcasm, and followed it with the cry, "Come, brethren, let us leave this infidel to himself. Victory to Mother Gangá!" He said this with a tone of authority, and moved away at once, thus giving an impulse which a Hindú crowd is very likely to obey; and they all followed him, leaving the catechist stand-

ing with an unfinished argument in his mouth, and a
half dozen boys staring at him. After only an
instant's pause, he began, in most simple language
and with winning sweetness of manner, to say,
"Dear children, if these grown men despise the news
of salvation, which we bring to them, do you listen
to what Christ says to such as you: 'Suffer little
children to come unto me, &c.'" And he went on
with the children till another crowd of men were
gathered about him, when he changed his manner, by
saying, "But this message is not to children only;
it much more concerns you, who have not so long to
live as they." And thus he introduced a most appropriate address.

This man married a girl from our orphan asylum,
simply because she was the oldest girl in it. She
was stupid, and of a bad disposition; and he was earnestly advised to avoid her; but he would have her,
saying that the Bible taught us not to despise those
of low degree. In this matter the effect of his education under the miserable social system of the Hindús
was very visible; he had no notion of the importance
of his wife's moral and intellectual character to himself. He married her, and it was not long till her
sordid disposition exercised a bad influence upon
him. He became depressed and spiritless. Then,
for the purpose of qualifying himself for theological
discussions with the Hindús, he read the Rámáyan, a
mythological poem of the Hindús, and carried it too
far; for he neglected the Bible for it. He began to
study medicine in the Hindú and Musalmán methods,
fancying that he should some time make his fortune
by it. We tried to reason and laugh him out of this,
but to no purpose; and it was not a matter for ecclesiastical censure. We at length noticed a considerable flagging of his zeal and energy; but he accounted
for it by saying that he was not quite well. At length,
on one occasion, he displayed a strange forgetfulness

of Bible history; and, as it was in public, he was
angry at having been found out. Examination was
made into his habits and state of mind; and it was
found that he had not read the Bible for a long time,
and had forgotten many facts of its history; and that
he had almost ceased to pray. He was more and
more angry at all efforts to set him right.

About this time he was directed to go out with Mr.
Owen on a short preaching tour, and refused, unless
a horse were furnished him to ride. Mr. Owen told
him that he should move but four or five miles a day,
and should himself walk. The man answered, "You
can ride when you please, and walking may be a pleasure to you; I consider riding a luxury, and will not
go out unless you give me the means to ride. Indeed,
I am not bound to go at all; I have worked here
ten years, and ought not to be expected to work any
longer. Give me a pension, and let me lie still the
rest of my life." At this time he was about thirty
years old. We reasoned with him, and did everything that could be done; and everything made
matters worse; an evil spirit seemed to have got full
possession of him. At length we suspended him from
his office and pay, because he utterly refused to do
anything. The same day he removed to the city,
and began to talk against us. After about a month
he went to Lucknow, and entered upon a negotiation
to turn Musalmán. Not suiting himself there, he
wandered nearly all over North India seeking employment. After more than a year he came to us, and
tried to negotiate; but was unhumbled, and we could
not accept him. He again wandered about, and in
one way and another caused much scandal—more by
his gross defection from the spirit of Christianity,
however, than by any personal vice. At length,
after nearly two years, he came back, and made all
the professions of penitence that could be desired.
At this time he professed no more than he did on his

first return; but his manner was much more satisfactory—there was much evidence that his heart felt the confessions which his tongue uttered. He was restored, and put at his work again, under closer superintendence, and on less wages. He has since worked quietly and steadily; but his energy and zeal have not reappeared to any great degree. We hope that he is "a brand plucked out of the fire," and that he will continue useful; but our high expectations of him are in the dust.

This story compels us to serious reflection. What could have persuaded this man to act in this mad manner? Either the great adversary must have had some special hand in it, to hinder our work, or the catechist must have been insane. But however it be, let us, in all confidence, even in the darkest hour, say, "they that be with us are more than they that be with them."

In the third chapter of this book mention is made of the fact, that some Musalmáns join us because their co-religionists will not allow them to drink intoxicating liquors. We have had experience of this in the case of one who, for a time, was with us, preparing to preach the gospel. During the Afgán war a clerk in one of the English offices brought a young Afgán into Hindustán with him. The Afgán professed to be convinced of the truth of Christianity, and outwardly embraced it. As often happens, there was much in his conduct to encourage, mixed with many inconsistencies. On the whole we had good hope of him. We taught and admonished him, and prayed with him. The blemishes in his character were mainly such as attach themselves to an aspiring and noble mind. We therefore had patience with his occasional manifestations of pride, and with his constant desire to have more income and to be treated like a great personage. By degrees he became discontented with us, went to Calcutta, and sought for a place, without finding any person to patronize him as he desired. Shortly after it became quite evident that his notion of Christianity was, that it would allow him to take wine genteelly after dinner, marry some pretty Englishwoman, and sink the Asiatic in a poor imitation of the Englishman. He got some patronage, until his character had become so much known that he lost the confidence of all Christians. He became Persian interpreter to a German prince, who was travelling in India; was dismissed from his service for drunkenness and defalcation; and afterwards I heard of his death as a drunkard. We must, I suppose, look on his case as one of unmitigated hypocrisy. We were certainly not to be blamed for receiving his profession of Christianity; and we did our best to retain him with us. We never perceived that there was any duty which we had neglected to perform towards him, and had nothing to reproach ourselves with in the matter; but it was a sad trial to see him ruined.

Let us turn to something more pleasant. A few years ago I wrote for the *New Orleans Presbyterian* an account of one of our catechists, a part of which shall be inserted here, without further comments.

"My friend is something more than forty years of age; though he has no means of telling his age with exactness. The date of his baptism is known; but the age at which he was baptized is not known. This may sound very strange to people in America; but the fact is, that very few of the natives of this country take any pains to remember the ages of their children. I have repeatedly known mothers to be unable to tell whether their infant children were six, or eight, or nine months old; and if they forget so soon, how wide may not their guesses be from the truth after the lapse of years. A very respectable man, as to station, and education too, has told me that he was about so high (holding his hand up to indicate how high,) at the time of the first siege of Bhurtpore; he knew, because his father was in the army then; but he could not remember, within five years, how long ago that siege took place; and this was all he knew about his age. Some families keep in the house a string for each child, tying a knot in it at every recurrence of his birth-day; sometimes they become neglectful; sometimes the white ants eat up the strings; and sometimes a knot gets tied in the wrong string, and inextricable confusion supervenes, and so the account is lost. Poor Robinson Crusoe made a mistake in his notches, and could never ascertain his Sabbaths with certainty, and how much less can ages be kept in mind by a custom so very liable to interruption! The *salgirah* (annual knot) is rarely tied after the mother's death.

"The parents of Harí were originally Mohammedans, from the North-west of Hindustan. Being in Dinapore at the time that 'man of God,' Henry Martyn, was chaplain there, they made a profession of Christianity, and were baptized by him. Here I will not lose the occasion to make a remark, to me exceedingly interesting. H. has often told me that from all he can remember of his parents, they were probably nothing more than mere nominal Christians; or at least but very weak and imperfect ones, making no impression for good upon his heart, either by their instructions or example. But they sent him to a Christian school, taught him to go to church, and thus at least served to introduce him into the ways of Christianity. The character of native converts is often very unsatisfactory; but here we have an example of great improvement in the second generation. The church ought to be encouraged by this.

"For several years Harí attended the school at Dinapore, till his parents both died, and he was left absolutely alone in the world. He had learned a catechism, the commandments, creed, &c., but remembers no religious impressions at that time.

8

"Being now a young man, with some knowledge of English, he went to Calcutta to find employment. In this he was not successful. But he formed an acqaintaince with a Mohammedan teacher, who allowed him to hang about his house, and to learn Persian in his school in every way he could, and thus gained his favour so far that he supported him about three years, during which time he acquired a good knowledge of the Persian classics. His teacher often sought to induce him to turn Mohammedan, but the grace of God enabled him to resist the temptation. His worldy interest would, apparently, have been greatly promoted by doing so at this time; and he rather wonders now why he did not; but he attributes his preservation, as he ought to do, to the preventing grace of God, though he was not at the time conscious of the influence of the Spirit at all, and felt no concern about his soul—supposing, indeed, that he was as good a Christian as any.

"After leaving his Mohammedan teacher he obtained a place in the office of the Adjutant of an Infantry Regiment, and then became an accountant of the officers' mess in another regiment. After he had left this employment, on account of some disagreement with the officers, he lived at Benares, where he had left the regiment, "from hand to mouth," writing English letters for natives, assisting them to keep their accounts with Englishmen, teaching a native gentleman's sons English, and the like. During this period, of several years, he hardly ever attended church, and did not know the essential doctrines of Christianity at all—at least did not understand nor feel them.

"At length a native catechist, belonging to the mission of the London Missionary Society, found him out, and took him to the Hindustáni chapel. There he was engaged by the mission as a teacher of Hindustáni, and received instruction as to religion. He remained in the service of that mission, in various capacities, till about three years ago. The truth seems to have affected him gradually. From his own account it seems that his self-righteousness left him by degrees, and he was brought to see his sinfulness and misery; but at the same time, the remedy was applied, and he was brought to accept of Christ in a way altogether different from his former mere wearing of his name."

After stating the way in which he came into connection with our mission, and that he was under trial for licensure, having studied Hebrew with me, the following is added:

"Hari's character is distinguished by gravity, earnestness, hope, simplicity, a want of confidence in himself, a shrinking from contact with evil, either in things or persons, which would anywhere highly distinguish a Christian man; and here, among the polluted, cunning, selfish, hypocritical, and dishonest people of this country, this character shines with distinguished light. His mind is of such a character that he can more fully use a limited education than any other man I ever saw. His strong common sense secures him from all pedantry, and from the mistakes into which another might easily fall. I trust him with the entire management of my Bible class. He is the peace-maker, the arbitrator, the father of all my establishment. He is my 'cabinet council,' and prime minister."

Another of our catechists has a singular history. He is the son of an Englishman, formerly a civil officer of the East India Company, and a Musalmán woman. He was brought up a Musalmán by his mother and her friends, till he was a young man, and educated in the Persian language and literature, receiving such instruction in science and philosophy as the Indian Mohammedans have current amongst them. His father was dead; but still his slight remembrance of him, and a prepossession in favour of the English, caused him to be discontented with his standing as a mere native; and he went to Benares, to see if he could not gain some advantage by joining himself to the English. An Episcopal missionary found him, trained him, and finally baptized him. He afterward served another mission as a catechist for several years; and finally joined us, accompanied by his mother, of whose conversion he had been the means, and who since has died in our communion.

This is one of the most dignified, polished, and gentlemanly men of my acquaintance. He has the good taste to wear the graceful costume of the East, and to continue in the use of the oriental manners, in which he was brought up. His language is most polished Urdú, and his eloquence as a speaker is seldom surpassed. I have known a crowd of Hindús so carried away by his eloquence, when showing them the excellencies of God in Christ, compared with their deities, that at the close they shouted glory to God. He is most useful in cultivating the acquaintance of native gentlemen, carrying on discussions with them, and exerting a good social influence.

Once an old man, named Harí Dás, came to me in search of employment, and told me the following extraordinary story, of the truth of which I afterward satisfied myself by such inquiries as I could make. I relate it here, because it brings out a good many points of native character, as well as some of the dogmas and practices of the popular religion; and, whether true or not in all its parts, the story is just as good for this purpose: it might happen amongst the Hindús at any time.

He said that while quite a young man he became entirely dissatisfied with the ordinary practices of Hindúism: none of them satisfied his conscience, or seemed likely to secure him a righteousness, on which he could depend. This is so common a thing that we often refer to it in preaching to the Hindús, showing them that they are always ready to do some new thing, because they have never found an object on which their hearts can rest. Harí resorted to all the ordinary forms of worship, and practised them zealously and abundantly; but they did him no good. He then performed all the ordinary pilgrimages. It was interesting to hear him describe what advantages he was led to expect from each, and how he was utterly disappointed by all of them in succession. Then, on the advice of his spiritual guides, he renounced the wife to whom he was betrothed, and became a *jogi*—a kind of religious beggar—and gave up all hopes as to the world. He had been told that he should find peace in doing so; but found none. When he had been several years engaged in this way, he arrived at a station where there were English officers residing—a kind of country town. Here he met a Bráhman, to whom he unfolded his tale of sorrows. The Bráhman told him that he had a Thákur [Lord,] who could do every thing for a worshipper in the way of spiritual enlightenment and help; that this Thákur was in a temple near the native town; that the worshipper must give a certain fee to the Bráhman, feed some faquirs who lived at the temple, offer certain flowers, fruits, &c., to the idol; fast and watch in the temple; bathe, pray, &c.; and then the idol would speak to him, and reveal the secret of obtaining righteousness and rest.

Harí Dás went through all the ceremonies; and, to make all sure, hired the Bráhman by an extra fee personally to attend him, to secure him from making any error in his performances. All were completed the third day in the morning; and the Bráhman told him to sit still and watch the idol till noon, and Thákur jí would answer him by that time. But noon passed without bringing any answer, and Harí went to the Bráhman and complained. The Bráhman said that since the Thákur had not been pleased to attend

8*

to him for his sacrifices and his prayers, nothing now remained but to abuse and scold him till he would answer. So the poor devotee sat down to this additional task. He called the Thákur all manner of bad names, as he had been instructed to do; he accused him of being a cheat, taunted him with want of power, and threatened him severely. All this did no good.

At last Harí Dás worked himself up to a real passion, through his indulgence in abusive language. He then said to the idol, "I begin to believe that you are no Thákur at all, but only an empty, ugly stone. There you sit, looking always the same. I make you offerings, and you cannot look pleased. I pray, and see no signs of your hearing. I curse you, and give you dirty abuse, that would make a gentleman crazy. I blacken the faces of your mother and sister in a way that would stir up a dead man; and there you sit with that eternal grin on your face, that makes you look like a monkey. If you do not answer at once, I will break your face with this stone. Do good, or do evil, and that immediately, or I will prove myself the better Thákur." And when the idol still did not stir, Harí in a rage threw a large piece of stone at him, and broke him into many pieces. His devotions, and especially his curses, had brought a large crowd of Hindús around the temple, who were looking on with much curiosity. Now they rushed on him with horror and rage. They did not care for his reproaching the idol: this they all do. But to offer violence to a god —that they did not expect, and could not bear. He would soon have been torn to pieces by them had there not been a station of Musalmán police officers at hand. They rescued him; but could not preserve him from the Hindú mob otherwise than by carrying him at once to the magistrate, who was an English gentleman. Into his office the mob rushed pell-mell, pushing on Harí with the police officers, shouting Murder! murder! help! help! The Bráhman also presented himself with a basket, containing the broken idol, and charged Harí Dás with the murder of his Thákur. The magistrate at first thought that Harí was charged with the murder of a Rájpút, who are also called Thákur; and asked what Thákur had been killed. The whole matter was soon explained, as neither party made any difficulty about the facts. The magistrate then asked to have the body of the deceased handed up for inspection, and they placed the basket on the table. He stuffed his handkerchief into his mouth, to prevent an explosion of laughter, and gravely looked over the ruins of the idol; and then told the assembly that it was a difficult case: the accused did not deny the killing of the Thákur; but still, as there was no blood in the basket, it might reasonably be doubted whether the Thákur had ever been alive; and, if it had been alive, whether such injuries would kill it. In consequence of this doubt he would postpone the case till to-morrow, and in the mean time would consult the judge, and learn how the law should be applied to such a crime; and they might come at ten o'clock and hear all about it. He would shut up Harí Dás in the jail. Accordingly he did send him to the jail; but in the evening rode over, called him out, gave him a rupee to buy food, because he had used all his means in worshipping the Thákur, and told him to be off as soon as possible, or he should not be able to protect him. Harí Dás walked twenty miles that night, and never heard how the magistrate and the mob settled the affair the next day.

This circumstance caused him to reject and renounce every form of idol worship. He took up with pure deism, but obtained no more satisfaction from that. He then determined not to wander about as a *jogí* any longer, but to secularize himself again; and accordingly entered the service of an English indigo planter as a clerk. This gentleman's establishment was at a distance from any English station; and a

Serampore Baptist missionary was accustomed to enjoy the hospitality of the planter when out on preaching tours in that district. At this place, Harí Dás heard the gospel for the first time, and says, that he at once perceived that it was just what he had been so long *feeling* after. After a time, both the planter and he were converted, and were baptized together. Until this gentleman's death, Harí lived with him; after which he laboured as a catechist in various places.

But during his long wanderings, he had acquired what may be called a predisposition to vagrancy. So long as his first patron lived, this was overmastered by his attachment to him; but afterward he could settle in no place—something always occurred to make him discontented. A second bad habit was that of smoking *gánja*, a preparation of the intoxicating hemp. Nearly all the Hindú faquírs practise this; and they often suppose the ecstacy produced by it to be religious feeling, and smoke it more and more. They esteem the reveries of this intoxication to be divine inspiration. Harí Dás was a slave to this habit; and his early patron had not taken due pains to point out to him the evil of it, or to bring him off from it.

It was some twenty-five years after his conversion when he came to me. He brought good certificates, and asked for any employment that would give him bread. I examined him, and was delighted with him. He knew all Chamberlain's Hindí hymns, and many more, and sung them well to native airs. The tears would roll down his wrinkled cheeks, when singing or talking about Jesus. With the consent of the mission, I took him as a catechist. He preached in a most affecting style. He was sent out twice with loads of tracts and gospels into the large towns near Allahabad, and I had reason to believe that he distributed them, and preached faithfully. During the middle of the day, when at home, he often came into the bungalow to play with my little boy, then about four years

old, talking to him about Jesus, and singing Hindí
hymns. The child was exceedingly fond of the old
man, and would leave any other play to run and nestle
down by him, and hear him talk and sing.

After a few months, however, he took a turn of
smoking *gánja*, which he had not before done since
he had been with me. Under its influence he did not
always talk discreetly, and caused scandal amongst
our Hindú and Musalmán neighbours. I had at that
time in the printing-house some lads from the orphan
asylum, who had somehow got a taste of this drug, and
were in danger from it; and we were therefore obliged
to deal sharply with Harí Dás, and to hinder him from
smoking it altogether. He took offence, and left me
at once. I regretted it exceedingly; for there appeared such evident signs of grace in him, that I could
not but attribute his ill conduct to occasional insanity.
I heard of his being afterwards employed several years
in an English family as a children's attendant; but
there he took offence because the family laughed at
him for wishing to marry an old widow, who lived in
the neighbourhood. He left them on this, and I have
not heard of him since. I have heard that on his
journeys he always preached against idolatry, told his
own experience of it, and declared that only Christ
could fill the heart. He used to tell me that he expected to die on some journey, and be buried where
no Christian would know of his grave; but, said he,
"Christ will know where it is, when he comes to gather
his people together, and make up his jewels."

Many years since, at a time when I had no catechist, a young man presented himself to me, asking
for employment. He spoke such beautiful Urdú, and
appeared so clever, that I was at once much struck
with him. On inquiry, I found that he was the son of
a gentleman, formerly an indigo planter in Oude, by
a Musalmán woman. He had a brother with him, and
both of them were married to Musalmán women; and

a young man, a connection of the women, also accompanied them. The brothers were nominal Christians, and the other young man a Musalmán. The one who first came to me was made Munshí to me, and his brother was placed in our English school as assistant, while their Musalmán friend was put into the typefoundry. For a time all things appeared to go on well. The Munshí was made catechist, and was an eloquent and persuasive disputant. I never have been so thoroughly captivated by any man as by him. But when some time had passed, we found that he was getting deeply into debt. Gradually we found out him and his brother in various falsehoods and rascalities, and were obliged to put them out of our communion, and discharge them. A pair of more thorough villains probably never existed; and the extreme plausibility that enabled the chief one of them to deceive me so greatly, at the same time fitted them to carry on their villanies, so that not a tenth part of them was discovered until the explosion caused by their discharge brought them to light. My disappointment as to this man was one of my chief trials as a missionary. This case should have had a place along with other sad ones, had it not been for its connection with the following.

The Musalmán young man did not seem to be involved in their offences. He had long been under instruction, and had made a profession of Christianity. When his friends went away we invited him to cast off their bonds, and no longer be connected with such disreputable men. He determined to do so. Afterward he was made a catechist, and laboured under my care for several years, giving general satisfaction. He has since become a catechist at Futtehgurh, has much improved as a preacher, and is steady and well liked there.

There are several catechists in the Allahabad mission, who were brought up in our orphan asylum. I do not think an orphan asylum the best possible place in which to educate men. It seems to produce a character always too much prone to dependence. For this reason our young men have not fully met our expectations. But they may yet improve. And as they are we have had much valuable fruit from the asylum. One went with Mr. James Wilson to Agra, and died there very young, but not before he had gained the hearty love and confidence of all who knew him. Mr. Wilson always spoke of him as one of the most lovely Christians whom he had known. The assistants of the Rev. Gopínáth Nandí, at Futtehpore, are from the same asylum, as are also our catechists who are labouring at our out-station called Bánda.

A catechist at Agra, who was under my care while I was stationed there, is a convert from the Armenian Church, a few families of which are settled there. He is a good and quiet man, very willing to labour, and of good character amongst the natives. He is supported by the Presbyterian church at Agra.

I have no doubt but that the details of this chapter will seem dark and discouraging to some readers. Many appear to expect that all news from mission fields should be rose-coloured; that all converts should be a joy and comfort to us; and that they should be not only free from the evils caused by a vicious education and corrupt society, but even from those inherent in human nature itself. But a moment's reflection will correct such an expectation as this. There is at least as much probability that there will be hypocrites amongst our converts as in the churches at home; that interested motives should actuate some of them; and that the natural evils of character, and evil circumstances, should mar the developments of piety. A correct view of our circumstances will even show that the missionary in India must have more of these evils to struggle with than the pastor at home.

It should also be remembered, that these anecdotes

contain no account of the mass of our people, or even of the greater number of well-behaved catechists. The use that ought to be made of these facts is, that the Church should be induced to give special thanks for those that are satisfactory, and to pray for special grace to be given to the missionaries and their converts, to guard them from ever present evils. If our history, a specimen of which has been given in this chapter, be compared with that of the apostolic period, we shall find a similarity greater than most people suspect.

Paul was obliged to reprove the Corinthians for dissensions, for disorderly practices, and for allowing a gross crime. The apostles had amongst their very early converts, Simon of Samaria, whose first thought was how he might make money out of religion. Mark departed from the service of Paul, when the latter certainly esteemed it a dereliction of duty. Paul complains of the Roman Christians, who were apparently frightened by the dangers surrounding them:—"At my first answer [trial] no man stood with me." False teachers arose in the churches in abundance. Demas loved this present world. Diotrephes loved the pre-eminence. But there is no need to go further: our work will be injured by the truth, in the opinion of no one who does not wish for an excuse for holding back from it; and the intelligent sympathy and prayers of God's true children will more than compensate for these defections, if there be any such. Let us all expect trials and disappointments.

CHAPTER V.

CHURCH BUILDINGS, AND PREACHING AT THE STATIONS.

THE preceding chapters have already made known some of our first expedients for places of Hindustání worship—one being the school-room in Mr. Wilson's house, and the other, a room in the printing-house. In Mr. Morrison's house the English service was held. This was a state of things that could not be otherwise than temporary. Amongst our plans would, of course, be schemes for building places of worship, in which all our associations would be favourable to devotion, where all could assemble with convenience, and to which strangers might feel at liberty to come. And we felt persuaded that the mere sight of a Christian place of worship would excite inquiry, and thus do good—that is to say, would, in a certain manner, be a continual preacher to the natives. The English congregation first took measures to build a church. The members subscribed liberally, and the other residents at the station helped them very handsomely; and a neat little building was put up and finished. I made every effort to have it built close to the native town, or in it, so that it would answer for a Hindustání chapel as well; but it was built outside. This was a miscalculation, as will appear hereafter.

The next year after my settlement at Allahabad the mission bought a new place for the families of Messrs. Wilson and Freeman, and for the two orphan asylums, on the bank of the Jumna, between the two parts of the native city. West of this place, or up that river, lay the old city—the city proper; and east of it, or down the river, a comparatively new suburb of great size, extending towards the Fort. The lot of land which we here secured, had a very large bungalow upon it,

9

through the middle of which we put up a new wall; and, after some other minor alterations it became two good houses. The former kitchen and buildings attached to it were so large that we put the girls' orphan asylum into them, with sufficient apartments for the matron, an East Indian woman, and her husband. Over against this place, but at a considerable distance, we built a house for the boys' orphan asylum. On the opposite side of a road, that was in front of the place, was a lot of land, that was attached to this estate; and on this lot was a building, that had been part of an old mint, abolished when the East India Company made arrangements for a uniform coinage for India, and for making it in the European manner. This old house we repaired, and made the place for Hindustání worship. The congregation now began to look like one: the two asylums had come together, and some other Christians were assembled. But this place was dark, hot, inconvenient, and of mean appearance. It was only intended to be temporary.

The English congregation, mentioned above, had been gathered in the first place by the late Rev. James McEwen. This gentleman spent some time at Allahabad as a missionary of the Associate Reformed Church, in connection with the Board of the Western Foreign Missionary Society. His health, however, never allowed him to enter fully upon missionary labours. He preached in English in his own house, and organized a church, consisting of some few Presbyterians, some English dissenters, and a few persons who had become dissatisfied in the Church of England. Two elders were ordained. When Mr. McEwen's health compelled him to return to America, the Rev. James Wilson took his place; and he was joined the next year by the Rev. J. H. Morrison. These gentlemen ministered to the Church, and were assisted by Mr. Freeman and me after our arrival. The people composing this congregation were almost entirely from two government offices. Not long after they had completed the building of their church, as before related, the government offices were removed to Agra, which had some time before been made the seat of the government for the Northwest Provinces. This movement totally removed this congregation from Allahabad, with the exception of the mission families, and left their edifice vacant. All the families of the mission save one were living three miles from this church; and therefore the building was useless for English services. It was also useless as a place for Hindustání worship; for, though not far away from the press, it was too far to be convenient for the native Christian women. The manners of Hindustan, as to women, are so peculiar, that decent native women cannot walk far from home, or go out in any other manner, save in close conveyances. English women act as they do at home, in spite of native prejudice; and no doubt the native Christian women will be able to assume similar liberty, when they can be recognized as Christians. Unfortunately, at present they are taken to be women of an objectionable class, and insulted if they walk out. This edifice was also out of the town so far that it did not attract other native visitors. It was accordingly taken down, and its doors, and some of its materials were used in the construction of the new church, near the Jumna mission-house, with the consent of the owners.

The mission desired very much to have a church edifice at this place. Our English, as well as our Hindustání meetings were now held in the old mint. But almost all of us thought it impossible to raise the means for building. However, as treasurer of the mission, with its approval, I began to "nurse a church-building fund," to use the phrase which was then my favourite one in describing it. The Executive Committee in New York allowed us to use donations received in India, for the general purposes of the mission, in any local undertaking of this kind; and we began to put all such accumulations into a banker's hands as an interest deposit. This Committee also allowed us to use a small sum, which we saved out of the estimated expenses of the mission during one year; and this was added to the deposit. When we had thus made a fair beginning we sent about a subscription, and the object was secured. This was a delightful labour for me; and Mr. Freeman zealously assisted me in it, especially in procuring the later donations to finish the work—always a matter of more difficulty than the beginning. He and I laid out the general plan of the work; I pitched tents on the ground, and remained there nearly a month, while we arranged for burning the bricks and the lime; and then I left the carrying on of the building to him, on account of the distance of my house from that place. He did the work well, assisted by my catechist, Bábú John Harí. The church is large enough to seat four hundred people in the close native manner. It is not a specimen of correct achitecture; but yet is pronounced pretty, and substantial, and appropriate, by almost every one. It was dedicated by a mixed Hindustání and English service, in which all the missionaries present took a part, in the presence of all our native Christians and many English and native visitors. The early day in our mission history at which this was completed, and the small means with which we had to begin, rendered our success a subject of much thanksgiving and pleasure.

Needing a chapel near the printing-house, in which the part of the church connected with this establishment might worship on ordinary occasions, I applied for a grant from the Executive Committee, but could not obtain one, because the funds were already pledged to other objects. At this juncture a friend offered to lend me a small sum of money —nearly enough for the purpose. The loan was accepted, and a fund for repaying it was "nursed," as it had been for the church. The loan was paid when expected—the final settlement of the whole account being brought about by a subscription amongst the native Christians. For this chapel we secured a lot of land facing the road leading through the large native village near the Press. This village is called Kattará, and contains the native shop-keepers, mechanics, and miscellaneous population attached to the European station, beside the original old families, which belonged to it before the English gained possession of those provinces. At one end of the town there is but a small space between the main street and the back part of the press premises, where the Christian houses are situated; and through this space a narrow land leads by the side of the chapel to the street. This private lane allows the native Christian women to walk to church; which is an important consideration in view of native prejudices.

Previous to the building of these churches, we built a small chapel at the *Chauk*, in which to preach to the Hindús and Musalmáns of the city, and for a vernacular school. This place was built entirely by a subscription amongst the European residents at the station. All Hindustání cities have what is called *The Chauk*, and some have more than one. Some are wide streets, and some are open squares, near the centre of the town. The Chauk is the chief place of business. The best shops usually surround it. Various hawkers of merchandize frequent it. The dandies of the city display their fine airs and dresses in it towards the evening. The tellers and hearers of news resort to it in crowds. Strangers go to it to stare at the people and sights of the city. At Alla-habad the Chauk is a vacant square on one side of the principal street. The back part of the square is bounded by a large tank, or artificial pond of water; and in the centre of this side our chapel is placed,

9*

with its back wall near the brink of the tank. The ground for this purpose was given to us by the government. Two sides of the square are lined with shops; and the opposite side of the street is covered with an arcade, in which are also shops. This large square, and the street before it, are filled every evening with an almost solid mass of human beings.

Near our place on the Jumna formerly lived an old Musalmán woman, who had been the wife or mistress of an Englishman. She had a house, and some jewels and finery, as well as a little other property. She became acquainted with some of the women attached to the mission, and was induced to attend the Hindustaní services, and finally made a profession of Christianity in our connection. After a year or two she died; and on her death-bed she bequeathed to the mission her property, a part of which had been already pawned to us as security for money which we had lent to her for her current expenses. She had no relatives in the world, and we had no hesitation in accepting the legacy. With it we built another chapel in Kyd Ganj, the suburb east of the mission-house. This chapel is on one of the main thoroughfares of the city. In it is kept another of our vernacular schools.

At most of our stations the missionaries maintain English services on the Sabbath evenings, for their own families and the few English who wish to join with them, together with that portion of the native Christians who can speak English. At Allahabad all of us usually took this service in turn, so that it proved in no way burdensome. It is an advantage, rather than otherwise, to have to preach occasionally in English. It has also been a great comfort to our families to have these services; for, though our wives learn Hindustaní, yet very few do so to such an extent as to render services in that language so edifying as those in English are. Beside this, the English service is profitable to our catechists and pupils who are learning our language. Since the removal of the English church to Agra a few pious Presbyterians have been in communion with us while residing at the station: one, a surgeon in the army, was made an elder, and assisted in our session; and after his removal to another station served another of our congregations in the same capacity. A few Europeans and East Indians have been admitted to a profession of faith there. In all these ways we have the satisfaction of knowing that our labours have not been in vain in the Lord; and that our success has, indeed, been eminent, when we consider the small number of people that were accessible by this form of effort.

When I was removed to Agra circumstances were such that I was called upon to be the minister of the Presbyterian church there—the same church that originated at Allahabad—for a year and a half. The Rev. Messrs. Fullerton and Williams gave me occasional assistance. We had three full services in the week. This has been the only occasion on which I have given up any time to other Christians than natives; and this by no means hindered my doing other work for the mission to a very considerable extent. Further mention of this people will be found in the eighth chapter of this work.

Beside thus preaching English in our churches, I have occasionally preached to soldiers of European regiments, both at Allahabad and Agra, and on the road when they were marching.

As soon as I could preach in Hindustání, I took charge of my own congregation at the Press, while the other missionaries carried on the vernacular services at the Jumna, and usually maintained a Sabbath morning service at the chapel in Kyd Ganj. The congregation at the Jumna contained the orphan asylums, the families of catechists and teachers, the servants of the mission families, and two or three ver-

nacular schools. The boys of the English school
often attended, as did some men from the city. That
at Kyd Ganj contained some families of poor native
Christians, such as pensioned drummers, and two vernacular schools, beside many occasional hearers. This
chapel, being on a great thoroughfare, often attracted
those who were passing, and was a good place for the
proclamation of the gospel. My congregation had
two vernacular schools, beside my own people and
frequent visitors.

The native infantry regiments in the East India
Company's service usually have Christian musicians.
They are native Christians of various kinds—the
greater part the descendants of the old Roman Catholic converts, left without any care, and very ignorant
and depraved. Many call themselves Portuguese, but
scarcely differ from those before mentioned. The Portuguese in India have mixed with the low caste natives
so thoroughly, that there is left scarcely any difference
between them: in complexion, and other physical qua-
lities, genteel natives of the upper provinces have the
advantage of them. Others of these musicians are
native Protestants, who probably conducted themselves badly in their missions; and others are the
descendants of the lowest East Indians, sprung from
European soldiers and low native mothers. Two of
the regiments are stationed at Allahabad, but not
always the same, as it is customary to change the can-
tonments of all the regular regiments of the line every
two or three years. Some of the musicians cannot
speak English at all, and the greater part of them but
imperfectly.

I procured leave for them to attend my service, from
their commanding officers, when possible. The catechists often assisted in efforts for this class. There is
no doubt but that good was done in some instances.
One family of six persons publicly renounced popery
in my chapel; but as this was near the close of their

residence at Allahabad, they were not admitted to full membership. They pledged themselves, however, to attend Protestant worship wherever they went. I also held meetings frequently at their houses. One Musalmán woman, who was intimate with the people of one of these bands, was converted, baptized, and married to a drummer. This part of my congregation was irregular, because some of the regiments were more inaccessible than others; but they often added largely to my sphere of labour.

At first, one Hindustání sermon in a week, and a Bible class, was as much as I could prepare for. After a time, a week-day evening service was added; and finally a second service on the Sabbath was substituted for the Bible class, and the want of this was supplied by exposition of the portions of Scripture read daily at our morning worship. Occasionally I exchanged with those who preached at the other places; and frequently Bábú Harí, the catechist, who after a time became a licentiate, took one of these services.

The different forms of preaching done directly for the Hindús and Musalmáns, are next to be described. It is with sorrow that I have say, I could not do so much of this as I desired. Having charge of the press, being treasurer of the mission, and often having much other secular work to do for the mission, beside being pastor of a small congregation, it was sometimes impracticable to find any time when it was possible for me to go out to preach for three or four days together. And often, after a hard day's work in an exhausting climate, there was not strength or energy sufficient to carry me to the city or the bázár, if there were time. Six hours' steady employment at a desk is considered a hard day's work for a European in that climate; and I often spent ten, and rarely less than eight, besides the duties that my family required, and all the time spent in actual preaching. Another hinderance, which I sometimes felt, was the want of a horse, to aid me in visiting the more distant villages. Walking to them, through the greater part of the year, is quite inconsistent with a due regard to health. And if one were to walk out and preach at a distance, by the time he reached home he would be unfit for the labours connected with the press or translation. Every mission ought to be authorized to allow to each man, who is qualified for this business, a horse and light vehicle to carry him and his catechist to their work. It would double their efficiency in this department. At Saharunpore, they have a kind of car drawn by one horse, that goes to the city every day, carrying the two missionaries and two or three catechists, or as many of them as can go. I neglected to learn how this is supported; but it is a good thing, and immensely increases the effective labours of the station. Sometimes the missions furnish a horse to assist the superintendent of the city school, when he lives at a distance from it; and this is a principle, the operation of which ought to be extended.

There are various ways in which we preach to the heathen. Probably the readers of this book have some notion of them; but still it may be well to bring them together into one view. For this purpose let us begin with street preaching.

When about to engage in this, the missionary and catechist take their stand in the verandah of a chapel, or school-house, or a place hired for the purpose, beside a frequented thoroughfare, or at the *chauk*, and resort to various plans to gain an audience. Often the catechist begins to read some tract aloud; sometimes the missionary accosts some man who is passing, with an observation about his health, the weather, or any common subject; and the people stop to listen. Frequently the people gather around of themselves, on merely seeing the party. When several are collected the missionary or catechist gives such a turn to the reading or conversation, that it slides into a continuous speech. When he is tired, the other takes it up. When sufficient time is passed in this way, tracts and Scriptures are offered to readers who desire them. Care is taken to see that applicants can read, and also that they seem anxious to get a book; except in some cases, when people from a distance promise to carry the book to some friend at home who can read; or a disputant is furnished with a tract on a particular subject under discussion, and which he may be induced to promise to read. The whole Bible is never, and the entire New Testament very seldom, offered on these occasions; but portions of them, such as those mentioned in the chapter on the press.

This is the course that all aim to pursue; but they are always liable to many interruptions. The hearers will often break in with questions and objections. When the questions seem to be put with a real desire to hear a more full explanation of any point, they are always answered; but if they are merely factious ones, intended to interrupt the preaching, as is often the case, they are evaded if possible: the missionary tells the audience that the question is out of place —does not refer to the subject in hand; or that he will be glad to take up the subject when he is done with the present one; or he hands over a tract, saying that that contains the answer, which may be read at leisure. But it is not always easy to get rid of a man who is determined to cause an interruption; he often insists on an answer, and becomes noisy. He perhaps pushes himself forward, looks to the right and left for support, gesticulates violently, and declares that he has floored the missionary, who cannot answer his questions; and it becomes necessary to take up the subject thus thrust forward, often to the partial or total eclipse of the original one. It requires a great deal of skill, good temper, tact and discretion, as well as information, to manage such a discussion well. A ready use of the native language also is most important in such cases. If the missionary hesitates for a word, his opponent will have all the more opportunity to push his objection; and he will generally be quick enough to perceive his advantage, and to seize upon it. To lose one's temper, to give anything short of a conclusive answer, or to stumble and become confused, are destructive of all hope of making an impression at that time, and will usually cause a scattering of the audience.

The temper is often tried by men and boys, who evidently seek a kind of notoriety by opposing the missionary. Perhaps he may be talking on the necessity of an atonement for sin ; when, in the midst of his argument, with a crowd of people listening with apparent interest, a Musalmán will break in with—"You believe in two Gods—you make Jesus to be God." The missionary takes no notice of the remark, hoping that it will not be repeated. "Oh yes, you are like the idolators—you make a man God." No answer. "You see, brethren, this preacher wishes to slur over an evident fact: I have said he believes in two Gods, and he cannot answer me." Then, taking courage, he keeps up a vociferation, till the multitude becomes confused. Here the missionary must stop, and answer the objection, or postpone it, or appeal to the people to stop it as irrelevant, which they will sometimes good-naturedly force the objector to do. But, whichever of these things may be the result, the opposer has gained his end, of showing himself off as clever and zealous, and a certain amount of hinderance has been thrown in the way of the truth. Or, probably some objection is made to what is said, and the objector will insist on having an opportunity to state it. At such a time if the missionary allow himself to be hurried into an answer too soon, the result often is a small running fire on both sides, which may subserve some of the designs of more formal preaching, but as surely defeats a part of them. When an objector seems to be very full of matter, and always has something to add as often as the preacher begins to answer him, and complains that he is not allowed fairly and fully to bring out his objections, it is frequently best to say, "Well, you may state all you wish, on the condition that you do it all at once, and then let me answer without interrupting me." If he consents to this, the preacher will then call on all the people to see fair play, and keep him to his agreement. Then the man begins, after promising that he will talk a long time now that he has the ground, and attempts to make a great speech; but frequently breaks down in two minutes. Thus the same man, who would have conversed and wrangled for an hour, is silenced by being allowed to talk as long as he will without interruption. Then the missionary asks, "Are you done?" "Yes." "You are ready to confess that you have had the opportunity you demanded, and have said what you wish to say?" "Yes." After this the preacher can answer him in quiet. If the opponent attempts any further interruption before that subject is disposed of, the people will generally insist on his keeping silence, that they may hear the preacher's answer. But now and then the result is different: several objectors encourage each other, and make a noise out of enmity and spite, and seriously hinder us. This, however, does not often happen: the speaker has often to deal with difficulties—seldom with impossibilities.

Sometimes the missionary and his assistant are obliged to take their stand simply in the street, for want of a place that may be hired for this purpose. I have many times stopped in front of a shop, to talk with the people in it; and, after introducing some ordinary topic of conversation, have been invited to sit down. The people readily gathered about, out of curiosity; and then I stood up and preached. At other times we begin, in something like the manner

10

of public criers, without preface or help, and do the best we can.

We almost always obtain an audience; but occasionally people are busy, or some noisy opponent disgusts them, or we make an unskilful and uninteresting beginning, and the people will not remain. This, however, seldom happens.

Our opponents are usually respectful in word and manner; but the reverse of this happens too, and causes great trials of patience. On one occasion, when I was preaching in the verandah of the Chauk chapel, with a good audience, principally Mohammedans, a man pushed his way up to me from the back part of the crowd, and interrupted me without preface or apology, by saying, "You are a liar and rascal, sir; you preach a corrupt book to the people. Hear, brethren; this fellow pretends that Christians are superior to us in morality, and that their book is holy: but in truth it allows a man to take his mother for a wife, and to steal." The suddenness and grossness of this attack both startled and made me indignant. I should be less than a man if I had not to confess that my temper was seriously tried. Therefore I answered him, in his own style in a measure—"You know that to be a gross slander and a falsehood. What induces you to be guilty of such conduct as this?"

He answered, "What I say is true, and you know it to be so."

I asked, "Have you read the gospel?"

He said, "Yes; I have carefully examined it; I know as much of it as you do; I have gone over it with great attention more than once, and am prepared to prove that Christian pretensions to pure morality are all a lie, and that the book allows the grossest licentiousness and dishonesty."

I induced him to repeat his specific charges, and then asked him to point out the places on which they

were founded in an Urdú New Testament, which I
held out to him. By this time I had quite mastered
my temper. He refused to touch the book, affecting
to be struck with horror at it, as polluting, and saying,
"Turn to the places and read them out yourself: you
will find that the seventh chapter and fifth verse tells
a man to marry his mother, if she be a widow, and
cannot procure another husband; and the sixteenth
chapter and eighth verse says that stealing is lawful
to a poor man."

I asked him in what book these things were to be
found?

He said, "In the New Testament."

"But in what book of the New Testament?"

He replied, "Now you are trying to mystify. The
New Testament is a book, is it not? What do you
mean by asking about its books? You are a tricky,
dishonest fellow. See, brethren, how he twists."

"Then in what *tract*, or division of the book?" I
asked. "You know that the book is made up of several small tracts; in which of them are the things you
have mentioned?"

He said that I was lying; the book was not so
divided; all he knew or would say was, that the objectionable matter was to be found in the chapters
and verses he had named; that I could find and read
them out to the people if I dared to do it; and that
it was all nonsense and trick to pretend that a book
had more than one chapter of a given numbering.

Then I said, "Very well; I will read those verses
aloud"—and I did so from the gospel of Matthew.

On this he exclaimed, "You are an infamous and
lying scoundrel. You are not reading from your pretended gospel at all."

On this I appealed to several men, who were
standing by, and told them that they had seen, and
at least partially read, the New Testament; and that
I would leave it to them to say which of us was the

liar. He vociferated, and repeated his tale. I knew
that several in the crowd were well aware that I was
right, and I calculated on their sense of honour.
And I also knew that I must do something decided,
or the greater part of the crowd would believe him;
and I was very thoroughly roused. Beside this, I
thought that this was the time to "answer a fool
according to his folly"—to "rebuke sharply." Accordingly I began, not on a mere impulse of anger,
but by calculation, to pour out on him a torrent of
rebuke. He tried to silence me by noise, and I met
him with noise—the only time that I ever entered
into *such* a contest. When he became silent, I coolly
repeated, that he was a black-hearted and horrible
liar. I showed the book, explained its divisions, and
proved to the people that he could never have read
it. I pointed out the grossness of his attack; and
showed from it that he could be no gentleman. I
reminded them of his pretensions to learning, and
how ridiculously he had failed to make them good.
Then I closed by saying that if *he* had displayed
the tendency, spirit and morality of Mohammedanism, *they* had better forsake it. The consequence
was that they refused to hear a word from him in
explanation; told him that he had disgraced their
cause, and hustled him out of the ring.

There are two things that helped to explain some
parts of his conduct. The Sunní, or orthodox sect of
the Musalmáns, accuse the Shias of holding the very
same corrupt doctrines, which he charged upon the
New Testament. This was the thing that suggested
to him the charges with which to interrupt me.
And there had recently been several tracts published
against us and the New Testament at Lucknow, the
place of this man's residence, in which the most gross
and reckless charges had been made; and he had
probably been reading them till he thought he had
such an idea of the New Testament that he could

appear to be well acquainted with it. Indeed, so shockingly false are these Mohammedan controversial works, that it would be no wonder to find in them the identical charges which he made, and the same references that he mentioned. It is a singular fact, that this man, after this scene, during his stay at Allahabad, attended my preaching several times, and was peaceable; and even called on me, and received the gift of a New Testament and some tracts.

On another occasion a Hindú said to me, "You are a great fool to preach about Christ. He tried for three years to gather a sect of followers, and when he found his effort a complete failure, he cut his throat in disgust." Another once said to me, "You have said to us that our gods are no gods; I should very much like to kill you." In this case a soft answer completely disarmed the man.

It is very common for us to be told that we are liars, or that an assertion of ours is a lie; but we get used to this, and do not regard it very much, though at first it is hard for one with the feelings and education of a gentleman to bear it patiently. We soon learn that a native opponent does not suppose himself to be insulting us by giving us the lie; amongst themselves it is a common part of conversation. And they all hold the doctrine that the end justifies the means, and despise an opponent who does not lie when he can do so with good effect. Therefore they look upon falsehood as a perfectly natural and justifiable weapon in argumentation, and can hardly conceive of our never resorting to it. They cannot feel confidence in the asseverations of any man, because they themselves are so thoroughly mendacious. They must have a good deal of experience of our truthfulness before they will consider a profession of it to be anything more than the greatest conceivable falsehood. This is at first a great disadvantage in preaching to them.

10*

There were two large villages near my house, in which I preached oftener than in any other near Allahabad. The cross-roads in these villages were good places in which to gather audiences. But we had to stand on the level of the street: we were not able to hire a place on either of the corners. It would be well to purchase corner shops in such places, even at twice their value. At Agra my experience in this respect was not different. I had three favourite places: two in frequented streets, and one at an old gate of the city, through which many people passed to get water, and to visit some temples outside. At both cities I sometimes visited the temples, and talked to the worshippers. Large audiences cannot usually be obtained at these places, except on festival days.

The other missionaries frequently went out to preach in the streets more than I did. I do not know that their experience, or their modes of procedure, differed from mine. I have told my own experience, not because I suppose it to be peculiar, but as a specimen of this work.

We often also preached at the *ghâts*. These are landings, or bathing places on the river bank. Some of them are flights of stone, or brick steps, built by rich Hindús, "for a name," or to gain religious merit. Other *ghâts* are mere slopes dug down through the bank to the water. These are good places to preach at in the morning, because all Hindús go to some one of them to bathe every morning, when it is at all convenient. Most missionaries frequent them when they can. It is at such places that women can be got to hear. They will not usually seem to attend; but if if one chooses his place judiciously, they can hear him while they are undressing, or dressing,* or pretending

* The Hindú women bathe with a cloth around the loins, one end of which is drawn over the shoulder, and covers the greater part of the chest. When they come out of the water, they hold a dry cloth of the same kind around themselves as a screen, and

to gossip. This is almost our only opportunity to preach to the women; though I have had an audience of them more than once, when preaching at a place called Alopí Bágh, near the fort at Allahabad. On one morning of every week, great numbers of them visit this place to worship a form of Bhawání, or Durgá, and to bring sickly children, in the hope of getting the goddess to remove her evil influence from them. But generally the women are very shy, and stand gazing at a distance.

Beside these, there were services at the Chauk chapel. It is common for missionaries, who have chapels in places much frequented, to hold evening meetings in them. They go to them at stated times, taking with them some native Christian friends, beside the catechist, if possible. Before dark there is preaching and disputation in the verandah, similar to the street preaching described above. When it becomes dark, the audience is invited to go inside and sit down, and listen to a regular discourse. The service on these occasions consists of reading the Scriptures, singing, and praying. The singing usually draws the people into the chapel very much. Then a sermon is delivered, and opponents are not allowed to speak; though after the service is closed, they may ask questions. I often went to our chapel at the Chauk in this way. This is in some respects by far the most satisfactory form of preaching; though the audience is very fluctuating—the people come and go without much regard to order.

Preaching in the villages around Allahabad ought also to be mentioned. This city is placed like Pittsburgh, Pennsylvania, at the confluence of two rivers; but only the fort occupies the place precisely similar

drop the wet one while fastening the dry. They seem to have no idea that there is anything immodest in this; and the men, who may be near, are never guilty of any rudeness to them. The customs of the country in this respect are admirable.

to the situation of Pittsburgh. The city of Allahabad is about a mile and a half from the fort on the bank of the Jumna. The eastern suburb, named Kyd Ganj, before mentioned, extends down the Jumna to within about half a mile of the fort. Above the city and station the Ganges approaches comparatively near to the Jumna, and then retreats from it, and makes a long detour, before they meet below the fort. Thus Allahabad, both city and English station, stands in a kind of peninsula. The village of Kattara, near which the press is, is very near the centre of this peninsula. Besides the two large villages, (forming in fact a town of some five thousand people,) that stand in the centre, there are about thirty of different sizes within three miles of the press. Some of these villages are close to the back of the city; some are on the great northwestern road that leads out from the station; some are on the bank of the Ganges in a great semi-circle on the east and north of the station; and some are scattered here and there throughout the area. The whole space, except the building spots and a few ravines, is covered with magnificent fields and groves; even the broad sand-banks, left by the river during the dry season, are at times fully clothed with a luxuriant crop of melons and similar articles. This is as great a field of labour as any one missionary and a catechist need, to keep them employed all the time: they could not visit all these places in the mornings of a month. Through this tract I preached as much as I could—not as much as was needed, by a great deal, but as I had time, strength and means. In some of the places, where the people congregated at some public sitting place in the evening, I went at that time; but the greater part of the places were visited in the morning. Generally I found an opportunity to gather a congregation before the door, or in the yard of some house. Often a great part of the people were absent in the fields, but some could always be found. One of these villages, about a mile and a half from the press, had in it one of our vernacular schools; and here I always had something to do when I could go. In these places we have to proceed very much as in the streets of the city and towns. The people perhaps are a little less disputatious; but then they are less intelligent also.

For some time I kept a riding horse, being directed by our physician to do so on account of a tendency to disease; and then I used to talk with people whom I found on the road. On some occasions this kind of effort was very successful as to obtaining hearers. On many occasions I have had very interesting conversations with people on the road. As specimens I will here insert a few extracts.

"A decent looking, well-dressed woman was walking near me, with a light walking-stick on her shoulder, from the upper end of which depended a small red bag. I asked her what she had in it. She answered me, 'My husband, Sáhib.' 'What?' said I, 'your husband?' 'Yes,' she replied, 'my lord's ashes.' Strange as this scene may seem to those who read this in America, it was not strange here. The woman herself, though grave, yet spoke calmly about it, and as if it were a matter of course; and of the many people who were near us, no one made any remark. I was touched with a strange feeling of respect for, and of sympathy with, the poor woman, though what she was doing was quite idolatrous, and could not easily clear my throat to carry on the conversation." [She was carrying the ashes to throw into the Ganges, her husband having died at too great a distance from the river to be burned on its brink.]

"14.—Very shortly after leaving the house, I overtook a man who was walking fast, and repeating Sítá Rám! Sítá Rám! as fast as he could. I asked

him if he wanted anything? He said, Yes; his land
had become very poor; he himself so devout, he
could not attend to his business; and his son so bad
a manager that the family was fast getting into debt;
and he was calling on Rám for help. I told him that
Rám came to destroy Rawan, and not to help poor
sinners; that Jesus was the sinner's friend, &c. His
attention was strongly attracted, and he promised to
inquire about the way I pointed out. Paid my whole
attention to him alone for this morning. He lives
about fifteen miles from the city."

"19.—This morning rode out on the Lucknow
road. A little way from home overtook a party of
two men and two women. Accosted them, and
learned that they were from some distance beyond
the Ganges, and had never heard anything particular
of the Saviour. Talked to them about him, and
having induced them to tell me something, which I
knew very well before, about their gods, I went into
a comparison of them with the Lord Jesus Christ."

"23.—Overtook three Musalmáns from the city,
and had a long discussion with them, in which they
did not hesitate to deny that passages which made
against them were in the Koran. Left them with
but little hope. Tried to get up a talk with a Hindú
soldier; but he answered everything with a full and
formal military salute, and a 'Your honour knows
everything.' Obliged to leave him without being
sure that I had communicated one idea to his mind."
"Passed on, and found a man and woman in the road,
who told me they were from the neighbourhood of
Cawnpore, and had come down to bathe at the junction. I asked the man what benefit he expected
from it; and he told me his expectations were altogether indefinite; he came because all the world came.
Are there not many like him in all lands—guilty of
folly and sin, because they wish to be like all the
world? He had never heard of Christ before. His

wife listened, but said nothing. Several others came up, and I talked to them till it was time to turn about for home.''

One of our special forms of labour is preaching at fairs. This is practiced by all our missionaries whenever the opportunity offers. There are a great many minor assemblages, all over the country, for religious purposes. The greatest of all is held at Allahabad, during the Hindú month Mágh, which falls in January and February. An immense multitude of people used to assemble here to bathe on particular days at the junction of the Ganges and Jumna. They believe that the Saraswati, which sinks into the sands before proceeding far from the hills, here joins the other two holy rivers, having proceeded under the ground. A full description of this fair cannot be given here; and therefore I will content myself with giving an idea of the way we labour at such places, by inserting some extracts from articles heretofore written on the subject.

"Every twelfth year there is usually a larger assemblage of people here than on other years; and as this is the year [1847], we were expecting a very much larger *melá* than we have had two or three years past; but we were agreeably disappointed—this melá really seems to be going out of fashion—bathing at this 'king of junctions' seems to be less esteemed than formerly. When I first came to this place the assemblage of people was very great—I well remember being almost crushed in the press a very little way from our preaching place; and four or five years ago it was no uncommon thing to be obliged to get out of one's buggy two or three hundred yards from the embankment on which we pitch our tents, because the crowd of people was so great that it was next to impossible to get on. But there has been a regular and great falling off ever since. It is amusing to hear the excuses given for this, at differ-

ent times, by the Pryágwáls [the Bráhmans who
attend as priests at the junction.]   One year it was
the Gwalior war; another year it was said, that the
pilgrims from the North and East had suffered so
much from cholera the previous year, that all the
people in those parts were frightened, and kept away;
and last year it was the Punjábí war that made the
melá so contemptible;—what they will say now, I
cannot guess.

"To what is this decrease in the attendance to be
attributed?   It would be flattering ourselves beyond
measure to believe that our preaching here has been
the sole cause.   But I believe that this decrease is to
be attributed to the efforts that are being made to
enlighten the country.   I take it to be an indication
that the preaching here, at Hárdwár, and other gréat
melás; at the several mission stations; and in preaching tours—together with the distribution of books,
has not been without effect.   I shall labour with more
courage—shall give out books more hopefully, as
long as I am permitted to remain in India, on
account of what I have seen and heard this year.
Last year we could not say confidently that the Sikh
war did not occasion the thin attendance; and the
natives told us not to exult yet, but to wait and see
the *Kumh* melá.   We have seen it—and it is not
near the average of common years, at least, five or
six seasons ago.

"Still let no one suppose that this fair was a
trifling matter.   It was far otherwise.   I went to the
summit of the embankment at the eastern angle of
the fort, which commands a good view of all the
melá ground, and looked over it.   The junction this
year is far below the fort, between which and the
Ganges is a tract of land measuring, I should think,
about a half a mile (more rather than less) by a mile
and a half; and this tract, usually destitute of all
signs of human habitations, had been covered by a

great temporary city, made of grass huts, shops of grass or cloth, tents, faqirs' enclosures, &c.; and circulating through its dusty lanes and avenues a multitude of people, greater than are ever seen together in America on any occasion whatever. There was no lack of people to speak to, nor of work to be done.

"Messrs. Owen, Freeman, and I, with our native assistants, have been in as constant attendance as possible. We had two tents set up, and have had constantly a congregation, whenever any of us have been there. We have addressed them about the character of God, and the worship he requires; about the character of man, and the kind of Saviour he needs; about the miracles, instructions, life, death, and resurrection of Christ; about the sin and folly of idolatry; about the evil nature and effects of Hindúism, and the beauty and glory of Christianity. We have made set speeches to many attentive and crowded audiences; we have sometimes conversed familiarly with some one man, while scores of others listened; we have read to them; we have set them against each other, and taken advantage of their division. In every way (except by pious frauds) we have endeavoured to set forth, illustrate, and enforce the truth; and O that God would 'set it home' to their hearts!

"Besides the services at the two tents at the melá ground, brother Owen has been attacking the enemy in flank, by having a service every morning in the Kyd Ganj chapel. The road from the city to the melá ground passes this chapel, and consequently a constant stream of people was to be encountered there. Brother Owen took Paul with him usually; and generally two or three old women, native Christians, who live near, were present. These women are Roman Catholics—have been drummers' wives, or something of the sort, and now live on pensions from government. Brother Owen says, that he

11

usually gave out a hymn, which he and Paul sung, and these poor women joined them, making a shocking noise, but one that very much attracted the passers by—better than a bell.

"I tried to take the people on the other flank, but was not so successful. There is a place called Bhardwáj, not a great distance from my house, where nearly all the pilgrims resort some time during their stay here. I tried to preach to them there; but the road is narrow, and was so crowded that I could not find a convenient place. Besides, a native band of musicians, with their frightful instruments, had established themselves close by, and made such an outrageous noise that I could make nothing to be heard, except when speaking almost in the hearer's ear.

"We have been assisted by the venerable Mr. Smith, of the Benares Baptist Mission, and his younger companion, Mr. Small; Mr. Drese and Mr. Ullman, German brethren, at present attached to the London Society's Benares Mission; and Mr. Schneider, of the Agra Church Mission; with their native assistants. And one evening, after the labours of the day, we had the pleasure to meet together, and dine and pray together, a company of sixteen missionaries, including the ladies. Thus you see we do come across now and then, a green spot in this otherwise barren wilderness.

"The people were, as usual, from all parts of Northern and Western India; and our books are gone with them to their far distant homes. And they will, no doubt, go home and talk about what they have heard, and think of it, and thus become prepared in some degree for the time when the light shall be brought nearer to them, and when God, in answer to the prayers of his people, shall pour out his Spirit.

"An intelligent young man from Bombay came into our tent, and introduced himself as a man edu-

HOOK-SWINGING.

cated in English. He was a government school man, and therefore knew nothing of Christianity. I had a serious talk with him, and he promised me that he would go to brother Mitchell, of the Scotch Mission, on his return to Bombay, and read the Evidences of Christianity. He was ashamed of Hindúism—said he was attending his father, who was on pilgrimage, but that he himself came to see the country; and finally confessed, with evident reluctance, that he was 'accomplishing the two objects at once.' He afterwards called on brother Owen, and had conversation with him, and examined the school.

"This man told me two interesting facts. The first is that the native Christian preachers, of whom you have so often heard as belonging to the Free Church Mission at Bombay, are most respectable men, whose characters even now are held in the highest esteem by the natives there: 'they think them deluded, of course; but not rascals.' These are his words, and contain a most valuable testimony. The other fact is, that he saw poor little Shrípat at Poona; and that he still wishes to be baptized. Ever since the Supreme Court at Bombay delivered him up to his relatives, he has been living separate from them—cannot be restored to caste. Let us hope that he will soon escape from the snare of the devil, and be assisted to make an open profession of attachment to Christ.

"Close to our principal tent was a tree, on which a swinging faqír was exhibiting himself. Every day he swung more or less—sometimes standing, at other times head downwards, with a slow fire of cow-dung burning under his nose. He had two ropes tied on a limb at some distance from the trunk of the tree; and at the lower ends loops for the feet, wound with red cloth. Sometimes he stood in the loops, and held the ropes with one hand; and sometimes slipping his feet through the loops, hung by the ancles. He kept up

the swinging motion by pulling at a small cord tied to
a limb near the body of the tree.   This man did not
seem stupefied, as one would suppose he must be, by
swinging with his head downwards.   We preached
the gospel to him, but he would not regard it.   On
one occasion a faqír of his own sect went with us to
him and ordered him to come down, and told him that
it was shameful to be making such an ostentatious
display of his devotion ; that if he wished to make
tapasiya he ought to go to the wilderness.   They had
a long wrangle between themselves.   We tried to
teach both, but with small success.   The swinger told
us that he was doing this to obtain sanctification of
heart, and assured us that it was a very successful
contrivance.

"I was witness to a very singular scene one day at
the commencement of this melá.   I went down to
make arrangements for pitching the tent, and having
gone down to look at the bazar below the embankment, returned ; when I found all the Sanyásís collecting on the top of the embankment.   Some Hindú in
the city had invited all the sect to dinner, and they
were gathering to set out.   They had several long
native bugles blowing signals, and I noticed besides
a great many other instruments—amongst them an
English serpent.   Silver sticks were carried in front
of the crowd, as before native princes.   They had a
very wild, and even frightful appearance.   Some were
totally naked; some were dressed in about six square
inches of cloth (in a narrow strip) and a string; most
of their heads were bare, with the hair long, matted,
tangled and sunburnt; one I noticed with long hair
turned backwards and plastered down all over his
head tight with light coloured clay; some had caps of
every imaginable shape, some covered with brass
knobs, brass plates and peacock's feathers ; some had
instead of clothes, light clay rubbed all over their

bodies; others only marks of the same clay on the body and face ; some few were well-dressed.

"This shocking crowd kept increasing for about a quarter of an hour, and then moved off towards the city. I did not count them; but I have often seen regiments of soldiers, consisting of one thousand men each, marching and manœuvring, and noticed the space of ground they occupy; and I fully believe that these men occupied closely, ground more than sufficient to contain two full regiments marching in close order : from this I judge that there were at least two thousand of them. I could not help thinking what a delightful dinner party the city Hindú had chosen to entertain. Whilst amongst them, I spoke about Christ, and they listened better, and were more mild than I expected. There were several boys amongst these people, and I affectionately invited them to come away with me and learn a better way; but I have often noticed that boys attached to these sects show a more hardened effrontery than the men.

"Several times it has happened, that when we were disputing with a Hindú, some man of another sect would take our part, and maintain some part of the truth with great zeal and ability. The common Bráhmans and the Kabírpanthís often contradicted each other; and one day one of the latter sect took up an argument, and conducted it with such ability—so completely prostrated his adversary—advocated so much of truth about the nature of God, and the nature of sin—that we were astonished, and could not help thinking that this man was 'not far from the kingdom of God;' but, alas! he was as much spoiled by 'philosophy falsely so called,' as any of them, only in a different way.

"We have reason to believe that some impression was made upon many minds. I noticed one old man, several days in succession, sitting and listening attentively. I asked him what he thought of what he had

11*

heard; but he denied being convinced.   Still, he evidently was much interested, and perhaps will not settle down into the same state of mind in which he was before.   Another came to me, and asked me where my house was; and said he would come and see me, and inquire further concerning the doctrine he had heard. He said he resided but twenty miles from here, and was often in on business.   I shall hope to see him again.   One day, when I was about to go home, a man came forward, and begged I would stay a little while, and answer a question.   He addressed me much as follows: 'I know that every man is a sinner; I am so; I have tried every way that the Pandits could tell me; I have tried everything that the Shastárs recommend, in order to get rid of my sin.   I was very early taught, that taking the name of Rám repeatedly would destroy my sins; and I began to use that name: day and night I kept muttering, Rám! Rám! Rám! and I was told by my spiritual guide, that as often as I pronounced that name, so often my sins were by its power cut away from me.   But when I asked how this could be true, when I found myself still so sinful— they told me that perhaps I had better try Krishn. So I called upon his name; but still remained sinful. I knew that I was sinful; I felt it in my heart.   Then they told me to make offerings, first to this god, then to that; but after doing all, I still found myself sinful. Then they set me on austerities: I tried them, and soon left them off; for I found myself more sinful than ever.   Then they recommended pilgrimages, and I have made three long ones, each of which I was assured had taken away all my sins; but still I was sinful.   Last of all, I was sent here to bathe, and told that this ceremony is of such power, that compliance with it will take away the sins of eight hundred thousand births.   I have bathed, and complied with all requisitions, but I am sinful still; I feel it in my heart. Now, I have just asked a learned Pandit why this is so; and he tells me, that beyond all doubt all my sins are pardoned, but that *the seed of sin remains in the heart.* I said, Tell me something that will destroy that seed, or keep down the awful growth of sin that arises from it. He told me, There is no such thing; as long as the soul is connected with matter, the seed of sin will remain in it! Now I have heard you—I have heard that those who really regard the Christian religion, become good men—pure from lying, cheating, the dominion of evil desire, and the like. Indeed, it is manifest that a good Englishman is better than the best of Hindús; and as for the comparison of one with the other, your people are immeasurably better than we are. Tell me, is there any place to which you go, or any ceremony with which you comply, or any austerity which you practise, or any particular mode of worship which you adopt, or any name which you repeat, that has the power to kill the seed of sin in the heart?'

"The poor man looked very anxious. I had listened to him in entire silence; his statement of his experience was so clear; he seemed to have such an uncommonly correct notion of the 'plague of his heart,' that I was unwilling to interrupt him. When he was done, I told him that we obtain neither righteousness nor sanctification in any of the ways he had mentioned; that the sinfulness of our heart does not depend upon our connection with matter, nor can anything within our power to do, remove it; but the grace of God is freely given to all those who believe in and truly follow the Lord Jesus Christ, to enable them truly to repent of, and forsake their sins; that the seed of sin remains in pious Christians, but that its power is manifestly broken, and day by day grows less and less. I then entreated him to examine Christianity; and told him he would find all that he had been so anxiously seeking, only perhaps in a different form and way from what he had expected. He promised me that he would

examine; told me his name and residence; promised
that he would see me again; and as he lives but thirty-
six miles from here, I hope he will.

"Beside these cases, there have been two Byragí
faqírs inquiring, but soon left. One Paramhans also
spent a night with our native Christians, and seemed
interested. But nothing, apparently, has resulted from
these cases. Many, very many, have appeared interested in a lesser degree.

"We have also had opposition: many Pandits have
entered the lists against us, and brought forward their
philosophy, and made objections to our doctrines;
and a great deal of time has been spent in combat-
ting with them such doctrines as that God is the
author of sin; that he is a sort of universal soul, and
speaks in all, &c. Now and then some saucy fellow
has bluntly told us, 'You lie, sir!' One faqír told
me, 'Sir, you come here and represent your own
deota (he meant Christ,) as perfectly pure; and you
blacken all of ours; you say they were all sinners;
and you say that your one is better and greater than
all ours. I am exceedingly angry at you, sir; and I
would much like to have the privilege of doing what
I like to you. I hate you very much!' And then
he gave me from under his matted hair such a glare!
I answered him—'Brother, if I hated you as you say
you do me, I would not take the trouble to come here
and offend you. It is love that brings me here.
And how have I offended you? I have set before
you a sinless Saviour in the place of those who you
yourselves say committed sin; for it is from the Hindús
and their Shastárs that we have learned the evil
doings of your gods; we say nothing of ourselves.
Come, accept the sinless Saviour; and then you will
love me as much as you now hate me.' He was
much softened by this reply, and heard with patience.

"Another time I went down into the enclosure of
the Nínaksháhá faqírs, and went close to their flag-

staff, and began to preach. They invited me to worship the flag-staff, and were very angry at me for refusing. Shortly after, they invited me to go and sit down on their platform at a little distance, which I did, and there preached. One man roughly interrupted me, by saying, I must not come there to tell them about God; for God was a lie! a dream! a thought only! I reproved him, and went on. Several of the faqírs were standing about, and grew very angry—two or three even went so far as to talk of beating me. At last they half courteously and half peremptorily invited me to leave the platform, and go to a quiet and sheltered spot, where we could discuss some point at leisure, and be sheltered from the drifting sand. As I was suffering from the sand and heat beyond measure, I gladly accepted of the proposal but the cunning fellows led me away through a weary tract of glistening sand, and taking their stand in an open space, where I could not endure the cutting sand-drift for a moment, asked me to say on! I begged them to go to a better place; and they said no place could be better—here was no crowd to interrupt us, and no house nor business to take up our attention—say on! I told them that I perceived they were making game of me; and as I could not stand such exposure, I would leave them, though I knew they would raise the shout of victory as soon as I should move; but that I wished them to notice that I was conquered by sun and sand, and not by their arguments. And as soon as I did turn away, they cried out, 'Oh! you are beaten! Oh! you are afraid!'

"We have not distributed so many books as we hoped to be able to do. Had there been the immense crowd of people we were led to expect, we were prepared for them; but now thousands of books we had intended for this occasion are left over for some other. We gave to readers only, and often refused those who seemed more anxious to get a large book than to learn what was in our books.

"But my letter is already too long, and I have no room for reflections. I would only call on all who read the *Chronicle* to render hearty thanks for the indication which the occasion has afforded, that the reign of superstition is in a little degree broken up. As I said somewhere before, I shall labour more hopefully now than ever. Our religion is recommending itself more and more every year to the people. Let us give thanks and take courage.

" *Postscript—Jan.* 30.—This is the last bathing day, and I hasten to tell you that the general appearance of things is much the same as five days ago.

"Since that time two inquirers have come to us; one at my place and one at the mission-house. It is impossible even to guess how they will turn out. I have set my man, who is a Bráhman, immediately at work, to earn his own bread, and shall instruct him. I hope many at home are praying for us here; and that their prayers will be heard, and answered in the giving to us of these men as a spoil torn from the grasp of the great destroyer.

" There has been a great man here from Multán, who had got up from Calcutta an immense quantity of cotton shirting cloth, and has given out to 25,000 (!) faqírs and Bráhmans five yards each. The day before yesterday completed his distribution. He gave also to each man about a pound of sweatmeats. The natives are wondering greatly at the great amount of *pun* (merit) he must have gained. Of course it has afforded us an occasion of explaining what is merit. But in spite of all we can say, the greater part of them probably still think we are distributing books and labouring for *pun* ourselves.

"The natives tell me a story about a native gentleman, that sent over a ton in weight of potatoes to one sect of faqírs here, (the Lungárís, I believe,) and that when they divided them they were only five potatoes for each man; and they were not generally large either. The consequence was, that the faqírs cursed him as a mean fellow, and no one supposes he got any *pun* at all.

"All the brethren from other stations left us immediately after the great day, but we are still labouring at the Melá as usual."

To the above I add a few extracts from an article published relating to the fair of 1850. So many extracts would not be given were it not for the fact that they contain information as to the customs, and opinions, and religion of the natives, that can be communicated in no better way.

"This year the mission determined to enlarge, and otherwise make more convenient, the tent in which our labours at the fair are conducted. The old tent was taken to pieces and reconstructed so as to be eight feet high at the sides, twelve feet in the middle, twenty-four feet long, and twenty-one wide. The back, and western end have curtains, to keep us and our congregations from being disturbed by the dusty wind. Behind the poles of the tent and near the back curtains was placed a wooden platform, and on it chairs for the preachers. At the west end, against the curtains, were two large bookshelves, with assorted Hindí tracts and scriptures. On the 9th of January this was set up and has been removed to-day. Since that day I have been there daily, excepting two days, from two to six hours, with my catechist, who has often gone before me, or remained after I left. My young men in the printing office have spent the greater part of the Sabbath, and of a holiday which I gave them, there, in assisting to distribute books. Mr. Owen and Mr. Munnis have been there with less regularity indeed, because they were obliged to keep the exercises at the school going on—but so much as to do good service; and their young men have been engaged as mine were—some of them also making addresses to, and conducting arguments with the Hindús most effectually. I am sorry that we could not all be there all the time—but the school could not be neglected, lest, after the demoralizing excitement of the melá, the city students should either not return to school, or come so dissipated as to be unfit for study; and I was kept at home every day longer than I wished by pressing business connected with the printing office.

"We are too few here. Three of us, when all well, and having nothing to attend to but our ordinary labours, can but barely carry on those operations that are constantly pressing upon us. If one of us were to become sick, something urgent must be neglected. And when extra work is to be done, as at this fair, it causes neglect and injury to all our operations, and is itself not well done. Will the Church have us go forward, or backwards? If forward, then she must speedily send out men to us.

"But we were not left entirely by ourselves in this work. Mr. Smith of the Baptist Mission at Benares, who has been here at every fair for nearly thirty years; and Mr. Small of the same mission, were here for about eight days.

"Besides the preaching in the tent, when several of us were present, some would take their places at the side of the road, behind the crowd in the tent, and there gather another congregation. Some took advantage of the shade of a tree not far distant, and soon were able to collect a ring of hearers. Two or three of us took our places together, and relieved each other.

"The number of pilgrims has been small, compared with what it was several years ago. It has been falling off for some time; but I do not know that there were many less this year than for two years last past. Our native assistants thought there were less. But certain facts afforded me much gratification. I will mention a few of them.

" 1. We have never been treated so civilly by the people as this year. Only two men and one boy, as far as I know, have been rude or abusive. One of them is an ignorant old man, a religious beggar; one the son of a Bráhman in the city, to whom I declined to give a book; and one a man who has some quarrel with the government, and supposed I was its servant. The people generally heard with the greatest attention and respect; and, even when they were disputing earnestly in favour of their own practices, were uniformly respectful.

" 2. We found many who were already acquainted with many of our books; and it seemed to me, that in this respect encouraging progress has been made.

" 3. Several persons attended at the tent for many days, and showed a great deal of interest. One read through one of our largest books, and talked much about it. Two others offered to become Christians on the spot, and came to my house to talk about it; but I advised them to examine the matter farther before breaking caste, as I was not satisfied with their knowledge, and had some reason to doubt the purity of their motives.

" 4. A respectable looking man told us that he had a brother at home, who several years ago received books, while on a visit to Benares. He said that his brother had never seen a missionary since he received the books; but that he had left off all the rites of Hindúism, and constantly told his family and neighbours that there could be no salvation out of Christ—prays daily to Christ, and is honest, peaceable and happy. I asked him where his brother lives, and his name. He said his name is Madan Mohan, and he lives at the village of Bhánrá, forty miles west of Gwalior. I asked him, 'Why do you not believe with your brother?' and he answered, 'I go with the world;

12

I have always wondered at my brother's singularity.' We do not know how many 'hidden ones' Christ may be thus gathering to himself, who do not make a profession of Christianity, because they do not know how to go about it.

"5. We have never had so many people inquiring about astronomical and other scientific facts, which give the lie to the sacred books of the Hindús. Many times I have been called on to state the reasons for believing the world to be round, and to show why we do not believe that there is any Mount Merú, or the seven concentric oceans; and also to explain the theory of eclipses. This is a most effectual puzzler of the Hindús; for their confidence in the Pandits is in a great degree founded on the fact that they foretell eclipses; and the Shástars, from which the Pandits derive their learning, are for the same reason held in the greatest veneration and esteem. But the Hindús are taught that the moon is twice as far from the earth as the sun is. Then, when we explain to them the true state of the case, they are much astonished, and very incredulous. But we are able to present the subject in such a manner as to shake the blind faith of not a few. Company after company came to me, telling me that they had heard that the English say, that certain scientific facts make their Shástars appear to be erroneous; and I took great care not to let the opportunity slip to impress upon them the reasonableness of doubt about the religious teachings of books that manifestly err in matters of science of which they treat. I believe that we in this see the influence of English schools and European science—even of the faint rumour of it that is spreading through the whole country, as the twilight precedes the rising of the sun. And it should be remembered that our religious books have not failed to refer to these scientific errors of the Shástars, and to call on the Hindús to examine these matters for themselves.

"6. Several of the lads from our school were present, at different times, and showed much friendship to us, in the presence of the other natives. One of them rendered me essential service one day, in trying the literary pretensions of those who asked for books; and he took up an argument earnestly for us, when assailed by others for helping us. This boy has to cross a ferry to come to school; and the lessee of the ferry gives him a free passage. This, for a Hindú, is great liberality, especially when we consider that the Hindús know the object and tendency of the school.

"7. I heard a great many of the Hindús speaking about the tax that was formerly levied on the pilgrims; and wondering how it is that now there is no tax, the attendance should fall off. Such seems to be the fact. It would appear that the bathing-place has lost something of its importance from being freely thrown open to all. Many ask if the tax will not be reimposed, and what was the reason for taking it off; and when they hear that pious people, through abhorrence of idolatry, forced the government to abandon its unholy gains, their astonishment and curiosity are unbounded.

"8. I do not know that one Pryágwál has ventured to oppose us this year. They are the Bráhmans who officiate at this bathing-place. Formerly, they used to come and order our hearers away, and curse and revile us; but they now seem to have a wholesome dread of the arguments levelled at them, and keep out of the way. Formerly, long rows of Pandits' seats also used to be seen, and they were generally surrounded by rings of people listening, who used to compliment the Pandits with rupees and copper coin in abundance. This year I saw but few; and one, whose table I examined, had only some small heaps of coarse flour and grain on it.

"I might mention many other little encouraging

circumstances; but these are enough for the present. It is evident that Hindúism is dying; but it is equally evident that with present means it will last for ages yet. And if the process of decay were more rapid, what would be the consequence? what would take its place? It is clear that there is no instrumentality in this country, nor likely soon to be, at all adequate to build up anything better in the room of it, if it were soon to fall.

*   *   *   *   *   *   *

"May the Church look at all these facts—and pray! May theological students look at this field, and come over and help us! If both these things be done, how soon shall 'one chase a thousand, and two put ten thousand to flight!' "

At a later date I sent the following letter to be published in America. It is introduced here because of its connection with the fair at Allahabad.

"I have recently received a letter from a friend at Jubbulpore in Central India, which contains the following paragraphs, from which those at home, who love the cause of Foreign Missions, will learn that the truth is working its way here in spite of all obstacles: and that in many cases there may be a work of grace going on where we least suspect it.

"'Can you let me have an Old Testament, or even Bible complete, in Hindí? I wish very much to give it to an old man, once a high caste Bráhman Pandit, who has flung off the faith of his forefathers and strives for the light of truth. He would be the first fruit for any man of God, who would establish a mission there, but he is weak in his views of things, and needs assistance. I think he has read just so far that he still risks a shipwreck of faith, and that to prevent this, a Bible complete is wanted. . . . . As yet he has read by scraps and odds and ends. He knows much of Old Testament history, and I have set him to studying the Psalms. He has many difficulties to contend with from man. His wife is still a heathen, and he tells me her taunts and sneers are bitter as gall, and of the grossest description; but still he keeps to her, and I believe from real love. He has one child, an interesting little girl about eight years old, whom he has taught to read, and instructed in the Scriptures as far as he is able. She is a very interesting child, and has an amount of character seldom met with in a native; and she apparently only requires to be trained to walk in the Christian path to keep it. Naturally very quick and intelligent, she has become more so under her father's tuition; and I should really feel most thankful if you could send me down a few Hindí tracts for this couple, suited to their capacities.

"'Strange to say, my friend the Pandit was first set to inquiring, after hearing a discourse, about eight years ago at Allahabad, where he had gone to do pújá (worship,) and to take a dip in Tribení jí (a title of the sacred junction of rivers.) He says one of your mission was the man, but who he cannot say; but the gist of the case is, that an argument occurred between the minister and some Bráhman priests, on their Veds and the Bible, in which they were worsted, and, as he himself says, 'myself shaken.' The old man has studied the Koran, and the Cazee here has made desperate attempts to convert him; but he tells the Cazee to let him know whence Mohammed obtained his laws, &c., so far as they are good for anything, if not from the Bible. If yes, then the Bible is true, and the Koran is made up of truths borrowed and lies invented, both blended to deceive.'"

"I will add but little to these paragraphs; they speak for themselves. But it is a great encouragement to us, who cast our bread on the waters here. Eight years pass in this case, and then we hear of the effect of one of our discourses in the old melá

12*

tent at Allahabad.   Each one of our mission, who
was there that year, may say, 'Perhaps that sermon
was mine!' and it is not likely that we shall know
whose it was till the end.   There is great encouragement in this to labour at melás.   In this case the
truth was carried three hundred miles.   Again, look
at the effect of the smallest influence of the Bible.   I
have never heard of a Hindú teaching a daughter to
read; but no sooner does this man take an interest
in the Scriptures, than his affections are directed
towards his daughter, as they never otherwise would
have been; his prejudice against female learning
vanishes; she acquires a character different from that
of other Hindú girls, and altogether there is a great
change.   My informant is a military officer, who is
not likely to be imposed upon.   His special duties
now are such as to require more than ordinary dis-
cernment and sagacity.   So we may feel a good
degree of confidence in his opinion."

The fair next in importance is that held early in
April of each year at Hardwár.   In 1853 I attended
at this fair, and afterward published a short account
of it, which is here repeated.   Having given some
account of my previous engagements, the article
proceeds:

"Being thus released from the church, I thought of
the melá at Hardwár as affording a place for labour
amongst the natives, the importance of which is very
great; and the expense of travelling in that direction
being much less than formerly, with the advice and
consent of the brethren I determined to attend the
fair.   I accordingly went from Agra to Saharunpur,
and from there went to Hardwár, in company with
Messrs. Campbell, Caldwell, and Jamieson.   I am
aware that accounts of the Hardwár melá have often
been published, and that I may say many things that
have been said before; but still the readers of the
Record are changing every year, and repetitions are

not always profitless. I will therefore describe briefly our proceedings.

"On the way to Hardwár, we spent a night at Roorkhee. This is on the great canal, which is being made by the government, to run from Hardwár, to lead the waters of the Ganges down the height of land between the Ganges and Jumna, for the purpose of irrigating the land. At Roorkhee large engineering operations are rendered necessary by a rapid fall in the land. Workshops were at first established here for this reason; the best practical engineers were gathered by the same cause; and this suggested to the government the idea of setting up here a college especially for the training of civil engineers. Accordingly a large school has been gathered here, consisting partly of intelligent and promising soldiers drawn from the European regiments serving in this country, and partly of European, East Indian, and native youths, some on stipends, and some supporting themselves. A large station has thus grown up, interesting from the fact that nowhere else in this country is European science and machinery so extensively exhibited and applied. After a cursory examination of this place in the morning, and a call upon the Principal of the college, we proceeded. Spent the night at the house of a young gentleman, one of the superintendents of the canal, and the next morning drove into Hardwár.

"I found this place close under the eastern extremity of the Siwalik range. This is a low range of hills, separated from the mountainous region by a distance of from four to ten miles, enclosing a valley, called here a *dún*, generally level. Through the eastern end of this valley the Ganges, after its debouche from the mountains, makes its way into the plains, turning the east end of the Siwalik hills. On the other side of the Ganges, other mountains closely approach the river, giving it the appearance of an opening through which the celebrated river makes its first debut, as it were, amongst the busy haunts of men. This pass through the hills may be considered a gate, or door, without any great stretch of fancy; and accordingly the Hindús call it Harí, (a title of Shiva) and Dwár, (a gate, or entrance)—Hardwár, the gate of Shiva, or, as some say, of Vishnú, for both are called Harí. The town is not large; I should suppose it contains not over five hundred houses of all kinds. The ground is very uneven, and back of the town it is covered in places by scattered trees and scrubby bushes. Everywhere are plentifully strewed rolled boulders of stone, brought down by mountain torrents. On the whole, it is as comfortless and desolate looking a place as one could easily find.

"We found our tent just being pitched in as good a place as the desolation afforded, a short distance back of the town, and near a Hindú temple, at which resided some religious beggars. About three years ago a man was carried off from this temple by a tiger. Some little distance from the tent, and close to the main road, we put up the preaching-tent. This has a large square top, with curtains hanging down, which could be drawn out in a sloping direction when desirable; and the sides were generally so arranged that we could be seen by those passing. Along the back part of this tent our boxes of books were arranged. Mats of a very coarse and cheap quality were spread down to induce our hearers to seat themselves and hear leisurely. The first day was passed in completing these preparations. The people had not begun to gather much.

"Towards evening Mr. Campbell and I walked through the town to the bathing-place. This place is not on the main stream of the Ganges, but on a lazy, shallow branch, looking dirty and disgusting, and, though spread out at the bathing-place to the width of perhaps six perches, not more than two in width a little way below. The ghát, as a flight of steps leading down to the water is called, is about the width of an ordinary street in a town in America, and consists of about seventy steps. Along one side of this passage is a series of small temples, the greater part of which contain only the filthy emblem of Shiva. We went through some of the passages connected with these, and stopped in a kind of balcony overlooking the bathing-place. Bráhmans had wooden platforms, on posts long enough to keep the boards a little way out of the water, placed in the river, where they sat to receive the gifts of the faithful, and to touch with their holy hands the bathers. Several people were bathing, many of them women. It was curious to observe the skill with which the women managed the slight clothing which they wore into the water, so as to make very little of an indecent exposure of their persons; and the nonchalance with which men regarded it all. We saw neither curiosity, nor impertinence, which might be supposed to be perfectly natural in the circumstances. How national habits modify ideas! Circumstances that in our country would cause women either to be regarded with disgust, or treated with uproarious fun and rudeness, were here witnessed without emotion, and passed utterly without remark. Here we commenced labour; we all talked with some of the people around us; and one of the native assistants made a regular speech or harangue, which was listened to with good-natured patience at least.

"The next morning we commenced regular operations: as there were four missionaries and three native assistants, we divided the company—two of us, with one assistant, and some books, took up a position on the bank of the river, where there was much passing and repassing, under the shade of a tree. The others went to the preaching-tent. Our usual course was, to commence a conversation with some one, and thus in-

duce several to stop and hear; then one of us began
preaching. When one was tired, another took it up;
and when all had spoken once, we usually tried the
reading powers of applicants for books and tracts.
Afterwards we spoke again; and when we had thus
spent two, or two and a half hours, we went to the
tent, rested, wrote letters, and talked; and after an
early dinner went out again, and did the same thing
as in the morning. On one occasion, Mr. Campbell
and I, with an assistant, went to the top of the bath-
ing-ghát and preached; but the crowd had by that
time become so great, and the noise so powerful, that
we did not think it the better place, though many
more crowded about us to hear, than at other places.
Besides the regular harangues, or sermons, as they
may be called, we had frequent conversations and
discussions. The time was well employed. The attendance of the people on the preaching was good,
and we had usually as many gathered around us as
could hear. There was, as there always is, a good
deal of coming and going amongst our hearers; but
generally the greater part would stand or sit through
our sermons. Some came repeatedly, a few to dis-
pute, and many with seeming real desire to hear.

"For nine days we followed this course. The people were increasing till the last: they would, however,
scatter away fast on the day that we left. Our last
day was the Sabbath, April 10th. We had a solemn
closing service in the preaching-tent; discourses were
delivered, reviewing what we had taught the people;
particular instructions and exhortations were given
to those who had attended often; and the services
were closed by a public prayer. As I stood on a
box, offering that prayer, I could not help thinking
how comforting was the thought, that in some parts
of the world God's people might be offering their
supplications in the sanctuary, and remembering us;
and I also wished that the time might soon come,

when churches and ordinances shall give the heathen
more opportunities of witnessing the decencies and
beauties of true worship."

I have attended several minor fairs, continuing
from one to three days; but the nature of our work
at those places does not materially differ from that
above described, and my space will not allow any
description of them to be given, beyond the following,
which is too singular, and too little known, to be
suppressed.

Behind the English station of Agra there is a
place of great Musalmán sanctity. They have a
stone there, in which they say is an impression of
Mohammed's foot. They call it Qadam ar-Rasúl,
the Foot of the Apostle; Qadam i mubárak, the
Blessed Foot; and Qadam i sharíf, the Honourable,
or Exalted Foot. The word *qadam* may also be
rendered *footprint*. The stone containing this precious relic is kept in what nearly corresponds to a
Roman Catholic monastery. There is a square of
about sixty yards on a side, the whole front a mass
of buildings of two low stories, and the other three
sides a high dead wall: this is the external appearance. The interior of this square is filled up to the
height of the first story of the front, and paved with
flagstones. The rooms in the lower story have,
consequently, no doors or windows behind, being
merely separate apartments for travellers who may
choose to lodge there, and are entered from the
front. In the centre of the front a staircase leads
up to the paved area. This also gives access to the
upper story of the front, which is divided into rooms
with balconies. These are for a higher class of visitors, and for the beggars who own the place. All
around the other three sides of the quadrangle, facing the paved area, are cloisters built against the
wall—a shallow verandah with little rooms. In the
centre of the area is a small temple, shaped precisely

like the most common Hindú temples, in which the
Blessed and Honourable Footprint is kept, and worshipped with all the ceremonies that Hindús use.
Not the low and ignorant Mohammedans only, but
multitudes of the intelligent also, worship this senseless lie; and, which is singular, it is an object of
great regard to the Hindús. Here the proud and
fierce monotheist bows down to a stone beside the
besotted polytheist; and the learned and the ignorant
hustle and push one another. Mr. Fullerton went
out with me, and we spent two days there at the
time of the annual *melá*. People worship there
at all times; but there are two or three special days
on which thousands assemble. We preached a great
deal. One of the days was Sunday, and we laboured
all the time we could speak. A singular circumstance that occurred here, will illustrate some of our
difficulties. We were speaking of the way of obtaining justification, and I quoted Gal. iii. 13, "Christ
hath redeemed us from the curse of the law, being
made a curse for us." The men immediately around
us were intelligent and educated. One of them
instantly said, "That is blasphemy: Jesus, on him
be peace! is the greatest of all prophets, save the
blessed apostle Mohammed, on him be peace!—and
to say that he was made a curse, is to charge God
with injustice and folly, and to treat the name of a
prophet—on him be peace!—with contumely and
scorn. You, sir, profess to be his follower, and yet say
such a horrible thing about him." I explained; but no
sooner had I come to anything like an expression of
the idea that he was the substitute for his people,
and accursed in their stead, than my opponent broke
out with, "Refrain, sir! I am well disposed to treat
Christians with some regard as 'people of a book,'
and you personally as one who seems to wish to be
civil and kind; and you must not utter such a slander
of a prophet—on him be peace!—lest I should forget

myself, and draw my sword on you, and you be massacred by my justly indignant brethren." Here was a dilemma. To be reproved by a Mohammedan for treating my own dear Saviour, whose cause I was maintaining, with disrespect, was something new. I had often heard the doctrine objected to; but never before had I known this peculiar turn given to it. I avoided the term that they objected to; but went on to talk of the doctrine of substitution, and to illustrate it from the Old Testament, till after nine o'clock in the evening.

There is a stone of this kind near Allahabad, in a temple like that described above, but in a much less sumptuous enclosure. Formerly it was venerated as much as that at Agra; but during the last generation the revenues have fallen off, and the heirs of the property have become troopers in the English army, leaving their shrine to neglect. But it is very likely that some one will by and by pretend a miracle at this place, and thus restore its credit, and get it again into public favour. This stone I have more than once examined. The foot-print is so clumsily made that it is a wonder that the most ignorant and unreflecting cannot see that it is artificial. The one at Agra I did not examine, because they would not allow me to go inside the temple with my boots on.

There are at Agra several descendants of Greek, Syrian and Armenian Christians. Their blood is very freely mixed with Hindustání, but they are still known by their national names. In the house of one of these I preached in Hindustání on Sabbath mornings. The audience consisted of his family, the family of our catechist, the servants of our own and a few other families, a few native Christians, and an irregular number of the Orientals above named. An interesting fact is connected with these people. Shortly after Mr. Perkins and his companions reached Oor-

13

omiah, in Persia, a Nestorian of that region went to India to seek his fortune, and has remained there ever since, residing at Agra for several years past. He has maintained a correspondence with his people at home, and received accounts of what the missionaries to the Nestorians were doing and teaching. The accounts struck him favourably. He had an opportunity in India also of learning what Protestantism is. Then he became intimate with the Armenian family, in whose house I afterward set up Hindustání worship, and told them so much about what he had heard that they too became Protestant. The children of both families are now being brought up at Protestant schools and churches. No facts could more forcibly illustrate the far-reaching effects of missions.

In addition to the modes and opportunities of preaching above mentioned, we are often able to proclaim the gospel to visitors at our houses. A great many used to call on me, and many interesting facts, connected with their visits, our conversations, and visits made by me in return, might be added; but this chapter is long enough. They who read it will fully understand our modes of preaching at our stations. It will also be seen, that the missionary force is at no place adequate to perform the work we have to do. It is my most earnest desire that one effect of this book may be, to convince the churches that, however much we have already done, it is still miserably inadequate to the great end proposed.

CHAPTER VI.

ITINERATIONS.

THE subject of this chapter is related to that of the preceding—both are on preaching, our main work, and that which is most delightful. During the cool season, from the first of November to the first of March, there is no difficulty in travelling about the country; and this period may be made a month, or even two, longer, without any very great inconvenience. During this time, all missionaries desire to do what can be done towards carrying the gospel to the parts of their districts which cannot be reached when they reside at their stations. The only way of accomplishing this work is by itinerations.

All persons who have read the journals of missionaries in Upper India, written on journeys for preaching, will remember that we usually travel with tents; and all will perceive, that when travellers use tents, their movements will be restricted and expensive. Now, as this book is written for the purpose of enabling all readers to understand our whole situation, and modes of action, we will first look into a missionary's marching establishment, and set forth the reasons for using it, and each part of it.

There are no hotels in India. A few at the principal English stations, on the main road leading through the country, are an inconsiderable exception. There is nothing like the numerous taverns on all roads in America. Two substitutes for them may be mentioned. The first is the Dák Bungalow, or staging-house. These houses are built by the government; and a cook, and one or two other servants, are paid to remain there, and serve travellers, who are charged each one rupee a day for the house and servants, and furnish their own food. Each room has a table, a bedstead, and a few chairs, but no bedding, towels, &c. They are built at distances of about forty miles, on some roads, to accommodate those who travel with relays of bearers, that distance being about what is convenient for one night. On some other roads, they are from twelve to sixteen miles apart, and intended to encourage travelling without tents by those who move with their own private conveyances. But they are often placed far from the villages, and are not suitable for the purposes of the missionary, who wishes to stop where most people are to be found. They are so numerous only on the Grand Trunk road and one of its branches.

The second substitute for taverns is the Sará—the caravansary of European travellers. These, in India, are walled enclosures, with huts around the inside of the walls. They are usually frequent enough to answer our purposes on the principal roads, if that were all, as no distance of ten miles is often without one. In them will be found a seller of flour and grain, one of wood, and some Bhathiyárás, or Musalmán cooks, who will furnish native food to any who will eat it at their hands. These places are generally built by landholders, who receive rent from the Bhathiyárás, and secure a considerable market for grain, wood, straw, clarified butter, &c. The Bhathiyárá derives his income from the fees paid by travellers. Every ox, or horse, or vehicle, or traveller, pays a trifle for being allowed to spend the night within the walls. Each person who takes an apartment, pays for that; bedsteads are rented, and a profit is made on food. We might halt in these places, if they were better. But the apartments are mud hovels, with only a door and tiled roof, hot, and disagreeable. The yard nearly resembles an American barnyard, and is used for many of the same purposes. It is filled with all kinds of people—riotous, quarrelling, and obscene—each cooking over his separate fire; and too often bad women and their visitors make up a large part of the company. A regard to either health or character will not allow us to occupy them. Thus we usually have no choice, but are obliged to carry tents.

The unsocial system of caste entirely prevents strangers from using private houses or articles of furniture. Hindúism utterly destroys every fragment of the virtue of hospitality; and so does caste-infected Mohammedanism, such as is found in India.

Sometimes the missionary travels without his family, when two very small tents will answer his purpose; but if his family be with him, the tents need to be larger. Those that I had at last were each thirteen feet square. There must be two of them, because it takes the greater part of a day to strike, remove to the next stage, and pitch one; and we cannot be without shelter in the mean time. I never had any doubt of the propriety of carrying my family with me, whenever its circumstances allowed me to do so. They, who are not acquainted with the effect of living in tents, and marching a few miles frequently, in the cold season of Upper India, would be astonished at the marvellous rapidity of the improvement that takes place in the health, after the system has been debilitated by the long months of heat. I am fully persuaded that, had not my health and that of my family been assisted by this process, we could never have remained in India as we did. It costs a little more than for a man to go alone, but not much; and it saves him from taking his horse altogether away from his family, leaving them imprisoned for want of it; and it also saves him from the expense of a divided household and two tables, which his salary cannot usually bear. Besides these considerations it should be remembered, that expeditions of this sort afford a missionary lady almost her only opportunity for moving about, and escaping from the monotony of a place, which, however long she may live in it, never seems

13*

to be home; since, however much attached to her family and work, her heart will always turn towards the privileges, the friends, and the churches of her native land.

Two carts are necessary to carry the tents. With one the articles required at night are sent; and with the other the food, table and its furniture, cooking utensils, &c. The usual plan of moving is this:— After dinner, about three o'clock, the dishes, cooking utensils, and day furniture generally, are packed up and sent forward with one tent. The cook usually goes with it. The boxes of clothes and tracts are so divided as to make the loads as equal as possible. This load is carried forward to the next halting place, previously fixed upon as near as may be, and probably arrives after dark. The people choose a place under some trees, or where they may find the best accommodation, and sleep without unloading the cart. This is done early in the morning, the tent set up, the cook proceeds to make breakfast acccording to an order previously given, and the table is set up, and the chairs dusted.

After the one tent is sent away in this manner in the afternoon, the missionary and catechist go out to a village; and, if they are not far apart, two may be visited and preached to before dark. Then they return, and find a tea-kettle singing, and some cups, and bread and butter, which are kept behind for the night, all laid out. The table is probably set up outside of the tent, and the stars look down on us, while the coolness and freedom of the open air, in such strong contrast with the hot weather and closed house which we have so recently felt, are highly enjoyed. After tea a slow walk under the mango trees, or on the open plain, as the case may be, or a talk with visitors, closes the action of the day. While the gentleman is gone to the villages in the afternoon, the lady has the tent transformed from sitting-room to bedroom.

In the morning the family leaves the ground early, in the buggy, and the catechist on his pony; and they arrive about the time the advanced tent is ready for their reception. Breakfast and morning worship almost immediately follow. The missionary and catechist then go out to the villages, and visit one or more, as the sun and the distances allow. When they return the cook will have got the catechist's breakfast ready. The natives all like to eat a slight meal about noon, and rarely touch anything earlier. The catechist will have his dinner—almost his whole day's eating—in the evening, later than we usually have our tea. After returning from the forenoon duty, we rest, read, write, or receive visitors, until dinner. In many places, all the persons, who have any claim to be called gentlemen, will come to see us. We then spread a thick carpet under a tree, and invite them to sit down; and generally have a long conversation on religion, and give them tracts and Scriptures. The head policeman of the neighbourhood comes, and requests orders, as to provisions, watchmen, or anything that we may require; though in most places all that he can supply us with is coarse flour. Schoolmasters come to beg tracts for their boys to read, and often bring a number of their cleverest boys to show. Their parents would be very unwilling that their boys should be Christians; but if they can save a few cents by begging Christian tracts for reading books, instead of buying something else, they will take the risk. Sometimes the tent is surrounded with visitors, and we are prevented from having the least quiet before eight or nine o'clock in the evening.

I ought also to say, that on many of these tours, a march is not made every day. The tents are pitched in some place where several villages are near, and the

gospel is preached in a circle of them for two or three
days; after which another such circle is sought for.

The furniture that is carried on these occasions is
all made especially for this purpose. Common tables
and chairs would soon have all their legs knocked off;
and therefore everything is made to fold up. In this
way the articles occupy less space. They are coarse
and cheap; for anything handsome would immediately
have all its beauty rubbed off.

This description of itinerating will certainly appear
very attractive to any person who reads it; but it
should be remembered, that all the complicated arrangements described are liable to accident and confusion. The stupidity of a servant, the breaking of a
cart, the sickness of an ox, and misinformation as to
the route, are constantly causing annoyances, that
need to be experienced to be understood; and yet it
is pleasant to go out in this way. On my return to
India, I hope it may please God to allow me to spend
all of every cold season in this work.

And now, that the whole matter may be understood
as far as possible, extracts from my accounts of itinerating, heretofore published, will be inserted here.
These extracts are somewhat numerous, because they
are intended to give examples of all kinds of our experience, together with incidental information concerning
the people, their manners and ideas.

"We marched from Futtehpore to Arapore. Here
we met Mr. C., who is taking up his children to Bareil-
ly. His wife came to Allahabad, where her relatives lived, last year, and there died of consumption.
Through the kindness of Providence, I was permitted
to be useful to her during her sickness. I trust she
was a true Christian before her illness; but she was in
much darkness, and doubt, and fear; and it was my
privilege to visit her many times, and lead her into the
green pastures, and beside the still waters. She died
in great peace, leaving to her friends a sweet hope

that she rests in Jesus. Her husband was with her the last fortnight of her life, and was much struck with what he saw; and his impressions resulted, as I think, in true conversion. I have had letters from him since, which have given me great pleasure; and the interview of to-day has been very satisfactory. He seems fully sensible of his sinfulness, and speaks with delight of the love of Christ. He is in a position to give him influence among his class; and I hope the good already done will by no means stop here. My conversation with him prevented my going out to preach."

"*Sabbath.*—Arrived at this place, Etawah, last evening. This morning early went to the masonry landings, of which there are several here, and at which many people were bathing, and read and preached to a good audience for about an hour. My preaching place was the platform of a Bráhman, who sits here to furnish worshippers with several little things that they require. He had a small stone, on which he ground sandal-wood, a little of the powder of which is often thrown into the river as an offering, and often carried, by those who have finished their bath, up to the temples of Mahádeo on the bank of the stream, to be used in a little worship of him, which they take occasion to do as they return home. He had, also, preparations of chalk and red lead for those who required to renew their *tilaks*, signs of the idol or incarnation specially followed by the worshippers, or of the peculiar subdivisions of their sect. There were metal stamps also, to assist in making these marks, many of which are too complicated to be readily made in any other way. Those who required his assistance gave him what they pleased—some a very little grain, some a few cowries, and some gave each a copper. He was very affable, and afforded me all the facilities for being heard that I desired. A Bráhman who stood by, took a tract at my request, and read a page or two to the people. A Nának-shâhá fakir took my part, and testified to the earthly origin of the Ganges and Jumna, when I asserted it.

"After breakfast went into the centre of the native city, about a mile and a half from the river. Talked to several groups of people; furnished a Mohammedan school with a few books, which the teacher promised to read and allow his pupils to read. Did the same to a Hindú school, on the same conditions.

"Several people came to us in the course of the day for books. At one time I had so many present that I went out and sat down in the shade, and had a good deal of talk with them."

"In the afternoon we went to a market at the eastern end of the city; but found that it was not frequented; and though nicely built, a failure. We walked up into the city, and preached to a very good audience near where we first preached here the other day. The audience were uncommonly solemn and attentive; the young man who called me an infidel the other day was present, and perfectly quiet, and staid to hear both Hanúk and myself preach.

"Thus we close this visit to Futtehpore. We have fairly proclaimed the gospel to crowds in its streets at six different points; carried on many interesting conversations; and given a tract or two to every one who appeared to ask for them earnestly, and proved able to read on trial."

"I met a man here to-day who had been a long time absent on a pilgrimage to Gaya, Ajudhiya, Brijnath, Jagathnath, and minor places. The man's mind seemed entirely dissipated; not in the ordinary sense of the term, but *gone;* his knees trembled under him, his eyes were bleared, the corners of his mouth fallen down, his power of attending to what I said, almost nothing, and his answers the most childish and fruitless that I ever heard from a man not very old. I asked him what the matter was. He did not know that anything was the matter—his mind, he supposed, was as good as ever. Other natives came around, and told me he was simply worn out by long travel and excitement—that the case was quite a common one, and that the man would never recover—would perhaps get home, dawdle about a little while, and die. Truly Satan is a hard master! And does not the case of this poor man rebuke us? Here was a strong, middle-aged man, who had forsaken his home, no doubt reduced his family almost or quite to poverty, and *literally worn himself out* in the service (as he thought) of God; while a very little hardship is 'a lion in the way' to us, who have so many more, and so much better, motives urging us to devoted lives!"

"About sunset, visited a new and handsome temple of Mahádeo, on the bank of the river. The Hindú Pantheon is largely represented by paintings in one of the verandahs. Saw here, for the first time, the Hindú cupid, Kám Deo, armed like the Grecian one, with bow and arrows, aiming at a woman in bed. Two female attendants, sitting by, are joining hands in entreaty to him not to hurt their mistress. This cupid is a big burly fellow, blue like Krishn, dressed most unclassically in a breech-cloth and turban. The temple is a very pretty piece of architecture, and furnished, in addition to the usual *lingam*, with a large marble image of Shiw, with his wife Parbatí at his side. These figures are dressed up in native fashion, with abundance of cloth. While I was looking at it they commenced their evening worship—the ringing of bells and beating of drums, together with the offering of lamps. Ran away, lest the lookers on should suppose I was joining in the service, or at least did not feel any repugnance to it."

"When we got to the tent we found it pitched in an old rice field. A glance showed me that, if it should rain, we were sure to be flooded; because rice is never cultivated except where water will stand.

But as it was too late to do better, we had to make
the best of it. Just at dark the other tent came up,
and we had all our people and goods together. At
this moment it began to rain. We made all haste,
and put up the second tent, so that all might be sheltered who could. During the greater part of the
night we had a very violent wind, but no heavy rain
till about five in the morning, when it began to pour
down seriously. The cartmen, the horses, &c., had
to stay out in it all.

"At day-break, we got up, and threw up a ridge of
clay around the tents. Got breakfast for ourselves
by making a fire in one of the tents; but the poor
people could not cook there, on account of their caste;
so they wrapped all the clothes they had around their
heads and shoulders, and sat down to fast till the rain
should abate. It began to rain less about eleven
o'clock; and I then, pitying the people, sent a rupee
to the nearest shop and bought parched grain, which
was distributed amongst them. All castes could eat
this, as it is not contaminated by touch."

"About four o'clock went to Ismáil Ganj, a large
village. This was a market day there. Made a great
mistake in supposing the greater part of the people
would be Musalmáns, and consequently took far too
few Hindí books. Found the people very anxious to
hear, and to get books. But the market was so noisy
we could not be heard very well, and we had so few
Hindí books that we could not supply the readers.
Preached as well and as long as we could, and promised the people that we would come again to-morrow
morning. Coming out of the town saw a man worshipping a Bráhman. Attacked them both on the
absurdity and wickedness of their conduct. A crowd
gathered around us, and we had a very fair opportunity of preaching, which we improved as well as we
could. Staid till the approach of night put a stop to
our labours. Walked back to the tent—very tired."

"Another class worth noticing was that of the faqírs, or religious beggars. They were of all kinds, though not so numerous as I should have found them had I come a few days earlier. These are generally sure to be at the melá soon enough, so that they may gather a long and full harvest. One day, while we were in the tent, I heard an altercation outside: one of my servants trying to drive away some one. The servant said there was a lady in the tent, giving this as a reason why the other should go immediately. He answered, 'Then tell them to give me something, or I will not go.' I went out to see what was the matter, and there was a Hindú holy man, entirely naked. I would not have noticed him if he had worn the usual narrow strip of cloth; but this fellow had not even that. He was one of those who profess to have overcome all natural feelings, whether of the body or of the mind, and to have attained to a state of complete innocence and holiness, and of consequent insensibility to shame and pain. I could not forbear putting his boasted insensibility to the proof, by pelting him with small stones, of which a plenty were lying by the side of the tent—very ragged ones too. He soon gave in, cried for mercy, and ran off like a deer. Had his nakedness been the result of misfortune, it would have deserved, and should have received, different treatment. I have had these men tell me, when I asked them who they were, 'I am a clergyman, (padrí,) the same as you are.'"

"We marched to Kassiya, where I received letters from Allahabad, and learned the melancholy news of brother Walter M. Lowrie's death in China. What an admonition to us all to be doing our work while it is day! I have no doubt he was doing with his might whatever he could; and that he is blessed in thus falling at his post, and being called early to his reward.

"In the afternoon I went into the town of Kassiya, and preached. I asked the people if they would re-

14

ceive a native assistant, give him a room to stay in a fortnight, and listen to him honestly, if I would send him. They said they most certainly would. I wonder if we ought not to employ our native assistants in this way sometimes."

"After breakfast this morning, went into the town and preached. Gave away a few books. The people heard with great attention. One man set himself up as my opponent, but had nothing to say, save taking up every assertion of mine and turning it against me by the use of the formula—'That is a lie when you apply it to us; you do so yourself.' I was at last obliged to tell him that one gentleman could not talk in this manner to another, at which he took offence and went away."

"Marched from Arapore to Futtehpore. On the way, learned that there was a melá going on near the road, under such circumstances as made it desirable to attend it. Accordingly, after breakfast, hired a palanquin, and went to it, six miles.

"The occasion of this melá, as the people informed me, is this: About two years ago, a large tamarind tree was uprooted by a storm, and lay in this condition till the people had cut away the top and the smaller roots. They say it was totally dry, though some of the roots were still in the ground. A few months ago, the owner of the tree set some men to cutting it up. They had cut but little, when the tree began to cry out, and the men ran away. A few nights after, at midnight, a woman of the village near by, having occasion to be out, saw the tree rise and stand up, crying, Alí, Alí, Alí! Next day, a Musalmán faqír of the same village took possession, and gave out that Hasain the martyr (one of the grandsons of Mohammed) had spoken to him from the tree, and ordered him to make a platform about it, and to invite people to honour it. At the same time, fresh twigs began to shoot out at the top of the dry trunk. The faqír says he asked what sign would be given that the martyr was really there, and was told that the blind should receive sight there. He obeyed the command; and as people came along, told them the wonderful story. Several blind have been made to see; people have had the places in which to search for stolen goods pointed out to them; one poor fellow, who presumed to touch the platform while he had swine's flesh in him, was deprived of his sight at the instant; and many other marvellous things are related.

"I inquired into all the circumstances carefully, and cross-examined all the witnesses I could find. I need not fatigue the readers of the *Chronicle* with all the facts that appeared: they were sufficient to show that the tree had never been dead; that it might easily have been raised up without a miracle; that no one could name or point out the men who had cut it, and heard the voice; no one could, of his own knowledge, say that any person had received sight there, except those who were interested in keeping up the imposture. The faqír family is the most important in the village, which consists of but five families, nearly all of whom are directly interested in the affair, and profit by it; and the others are very low people, who might be easily hired to aid in this or any other rascality, as they are professed thieves. In short, the tree has evidently been set up by these people, for the sake of the contributions that are now coming in, and a few people have been suborned to give false evidence, and the credulity of others has been wrought upon, till the thing has grown to the present height. A melá is held every Thursday: sweetmeat-makers, grain-sellers, toymen, and some others, make a good thing out of it, and are all interested in the continuance of the fraud. Both Mohammedans and Hindús frequent the place, and equally believe in the power of the saint.

"I took up the platform as a preaching place; and though doubtful whether they would permit me to remain there, I thought it best to try, as anything I might say against the imposture on its very seat, would be more likely to have effect, than if said at any other place. I talked there as long as I could endure the heat, and then went under the shade of a tree. A great crowd followed me; and those that were behind compelled those who were nearest me to sit down, so that they might hear better. I talked as long as I had strength, on the insufficiency of their religion to satisfy the heart, as illustrated by their readiness to run after every new thing, even to the stock of an old tamarind tree; and then told them how the heart could rest on the perfect atonement of Christ, when once it was renewed by faith. Afterwards I distributed several tracts, and conversed with three or four small groups, and then left for the tent.

"After leaving the ground, I met Hanúk, who, having reached the tent after I went from it, had followed me. This doubled my talking power, and I turned back with him. We went on the platform of this new idol; and from thence Hanúk denounced, with a great appearance of indignation, the idolatry and rascality of the whole affair. Then he melted with pity for the people, and begged them to come to Christ, who would keep them from all such folly. Then he again turned upon the faqír, and denounced upon him the anger and curse of a jealous God, for his proceedings. I joined him in this; and we left the poor people confounded and speechless. Then we asked the people to come into the shade with us; and there again told of the love, power, and glory of Christ. We reached home just as it was growing dark, very much fatigued.

"This is the second new idol that I have encountered during this short journey; and they are frequented by thousands. There were not less than a thousand people present to-day, and I met a great number going away. Facts of this kind show the spiritual state of the people in a more striking and melancholy light than even their observance of the old idolatry. That has at least antiquity in its favour; but here we see people running eagerly after every new lie; straining to believe the most improbable pretensions; asking for no proof; freely offering money, grain, and clothes, on the shrine of every new abomination, while our message of truth is heard with indifference. We have no lying wonders, with which to captivate their gross senses. And the great body of the Musalmáns are as deep in this mire as the Hindús; saying there is but one God, but running after Hindú idols, on the pretence that God can work by any instrument he pleases. They know nothing of the sublime declaration, 'My glory will I not give to another.'

"They showed me a girl, who, they said, had been made to see a little with one eye to-day. A man held up a finger, and asked how many there were. She answered, one. He held up two; and she said two— and so on regularly to five. Then I pushed him away, and held up my doubled fist, and asked her how many fingers were open. She answered, *two!* Her mother picked up an old flower, and asked her to tell what it was. She said, a flower. Then I made them all hold their tongues, and showed her a piece of white sweetmeat, and asked her what it was. She said it was *a flower!* Really I never saw so awkward and transparent a deception in my life; and yet the people were all agog for swallowing it, and seemed sorry that I had overthrown the credit of the lying blind girl."

"I find to-day that a Hindú servant now with me regards the Sabbath. He cooks his dinner with more than common neatness and care, and uses no salt. On other days he eats with less care, and puts salt in his food. He does not know any reason why he makes this difference, except that it is the custom of his caste."

"By this time five or six men were following me
14*

with some appearance of interest. I found a man sitting on a small bedstead in front of a room, having beside him an English fowling-piece, a native matchlock gun, and a blunderbuss—in his belt a pistol, and across his knees a sword. A nice horse was tethered near him. I saw he was a man of some consequence, as I might safely calculate the number of his servants by the arms I saw near him. I addressed him by the title of 'Their Excellency,' as it is the custom to give high-sounding titles, and in the third person plural; and he bestowed upon me the title 'Majesty,' and invited me to take a seat on his bedstead. He told me he was a native lawyer. I commenced telling him about Christ, and he asked me why we eat pork. I told him that was a matter of merely temporal concern, but the salvation of the soul related to eternity. But why do you consider wine allowable? I begged him not to introduce a matter of so little consequence; told him that, now there were several Hindús listening, it became a Christian and a Musalmán to converse on such subjects as would tend to show them a better way than idolatry. But why do not your people wear beards? Because, with reference to mere external matters, concerning which God has given us no directions, and about which he does not care, we do just what is most convenient; the soul is of more importance. Pardon me—I must look further, and find some one to talk with who cares for his soul. I made him an obeisance, and he rose up very politely to return it; but as if the spirit of trifling formality had fully possessed him, he asked me, How dare you pray with your body dirty? Your people go and worship before they bathe. By this time all my listeners were gone."

"Preached here to eight men, and gave them two tracts. They had never heard a word of the gospel before. I spent a considerable time with them, and they followed me to the bottom of the bank, and offered to furnish me with anything they could to eat."

"*Sabbath.*—Moved the boat about a mile this morning in order to reach Músánagar (city of Moses,) which we could not do last evening. After breakfast walked to the city, nearly a mile, through the wildest place I have ever seen in this country. The whole region between the town and the river, as far as the eye can reach up and down the stream, is cut up into the most ugly ravines, the residence, as the people tell me, of tigers and wolves. Near the river the ground is higher than elsewhere, and full of broken bricks— the tradition concerning which is, that *thousands* of years ago there was a fort here. Walked into the town with a man, who offered to introduce me to the principal Pandit, which he did. They gave me a seat in a pleasant shade; and we had a long and interesting conversation in the presence of a good and attentive audience."

"We came down into the town and preached to a considerable company of Musalmáns. They offered me paun to eat, and a pipe; both of which I declined on the ground that they would hinder my talking.

"On the way back, stopped to examine the spot where a new Bhawání (a goddess of that name) has recently made her appearance. The people told us she appeared to a Bráhman in a dream, and told him where to dig to find her. I told them that no one could find so readily as he who hides; and that it was very easy to pretend to have a dream. The whole thing is a contemptible little image of an ugly woman, about eight inches high, shrined in a new temple about one-fourth the size of a dog kennel. Doubtless it is a good speculation for the Bráhman, as the place seems to have been much frequented.

"In returning through the town of Daranagar we discovered an Albino, a man of the Kalwár, or distiller caste. He would have been perfectly white had not his skin acquired a reddish raw-looking shade—hair white, and eyes red, like those of a white rabbit. He was a very disagreeable object. He told us he was married and had a son of the usual India ink colour. He said his health was usually good, though his eyes could ill bear a strong light. He had once a brother like himself, who is now dead.

"Near this same town we stumbled on a marked specimen of the people's taste in modelling and sculpture—the colossal figure of a man, or of one of the Deotás. The figure was lying on its stomach, the legs extending out behind, the arms spread out from the sides, but inclining backwards, and the head and breast elevated, as if to peep over a wall before it, for the purpose of stealing a fearful look at an image of Ráwan and his children, who were standing in the majesty of painted clay, at the further side of a field. The work was too large to be the mere play of the boys, and too silly to be done by any but the most childish men. In itself the thing was highly ludicrous; but when we consider that it is gravely connected with the religion of the people, it becomes very painful.

"4.—A day of hard work, and of few events. Preached in Kara, in two places, a long time. The people wanted to make a feast for me, and consulted me about what would be most agreeable; but I told them I was most sensible of their kindness, and would rather accept of their offer than appear ungrateful; still I did not wish to give them trouble, and would respectfully request they would say no more about it.

5.—Went to Daranagar, and preached in two places. Had the greatest crowd about us that we have yet had. Nothing particular occurred, except a discussion about the Bhawání, which has recently come out of the ground here, mentioned under date of the 3d. It never seems to have occurred to any of the people here, that the Bráhman might have hid the image

where he afterwards pretended to find it—I trust we
have done something to damage his profits.

"As we were coming out of the town an old Bráhman hailed me, and asked if he should get his support
from us if he should come with us. I asked him why •
he and the most of the people always had that subject
uppermost, and were always thinking of their belly.
He answered, that a man could do nothing without
eating; and that if he could fill his belly by it, he
would worship God, or Bhawání, or Jesus. I added,
or Satan. And telling him we had no use for such
converts, no object in making them, and no desire to
see them, and that such conversion could do men no
good, I abruptly turned away from him. Then I
told the people that we sought their future happi-
ness, and had no desire to detach them from their
business or their fields; I invited them to receive
Christ for his own sake, and for the life to come; and
not for worldly advantage. The scene made an evident impression.

"I noticed to-day more of that fatal levity in treating religious subjects, which has often been noticed in
the Hindús, than I have seen before in a long time.
But it really is not strange that the Hindús should
treat the most serious subjects with a degree of light-
ness perfectly inconceivable to those who have not
witnessed it. Their two greatest amusements are,
their religious festivals, and listening to their religious
traditions. The chief festivals are the Húlí—throwing dirt over each other, and singing licentious songs;
making a large image of Ráwan, and blowing him up;
setting up two boys as Rám and Lakshman, and con-
necting dancing, juggler's tricks, and masquerading
with it; and the like. Their traditions are of the impure and ludicrous intrigues and adventures of the
gods; and to impious people tales of impurity always
seem funny; so that whenever we begin to talk about
Christianity they seem to be set all agog with the ex-

pectation that something is coming which will prove equivalent to a good joke. Poor people! they are never serious themselves about religion, and they can hardly conceive how we can be so. It takes a long acquaintance to overcome this levity; and when it is overcome, it is succeeded, not by interest, but by weariness; because the subject of course is, to such minds, one of the most dull and dreary that could be imagined—there is no *fun* in it—and faith has not come in, to give its dread truths any effect on their minds.

"After breakfast I took some tracts and went to the encampment of a company of native artillery near by. There were both Musalmáns and Hindús. I had a long talk with them, and gave away four tracts.

"Nearly all the men were away in the fields. I found only three to speak to. The women all either ran into their houses or peeped at me from the distance. Before some of the doors were little conical heaps of cow-dung with a tuft of grass stuck in the top. A little wall of the same material surrounded the heap; and both were covered over with little spots of cotton-wool. This they told me was a kind of altar for the worship of the cows and oxen, which is celebrated once in a year. They gave no reason for this worship, except the usefulness of these animals. For the same reason, a few evenings since, our skipper worshipped the boat, offering a lamp to its figurehead.

"29th.—Preached in the evening at a village. In the moonlight after tea sat on deck listening to the sound of the Musalmán drums celebrating the Muhurram in one village, and to the drum symphony of a Hindú story-teller in another. Shortly our own boatmen set up a tune with a drum accompaniment. The scene was beautiful; and yet the whole air was filled with Satan's music. When shall it be filled

with the sound of psalms and Christian family
worship!"

"Went from this village to a smaller one—had
eight men, two women, and some boys to hear us.
The people were very stupid and ignorant. We
found it difficult to talk small enough to make them
understand anything. Did as well as we could; and
they were evidently gratified by our attempts,
whether any other good were effected or not. They
all promised me that they would instantly forsake
Hindúism, and seek Christ. This kind of promise is
not uncommon; but fulfilment, alas! is very rare."

"This morning passed a village, which was burnt
about eight days ago. The cattle and people looked
desolate enough amongst the fire-marked clay walls
without roofs and doors. The roofs in this region,
being merely a thin thatch of grass on very slender
poles, soon are entirely destroyed by fire; and the
houses are always so huddled together, that when one
roof flames, the village is gone. But the people will
soon cover in their houses again in some way, and sit
down content. It is certain that after the fire was
once over they troubled themselves very little about it.
Truly, there is some consolation in having little to
lose, and in an apathy that can submit to anything.
But what can be done for a people so *quiet?*"

"Went to a village called Brahmanpur, about two
miles off, and preached a good while to about a dozen
Hindús, who heard well. Most of the people were
out in the fields at their work, and we at first thought
we should find none to talk to; but we walked all
through the town, inviting one after another to follow
us, and at last stopped on the border of the tank or
reservoir, under the shade of a tree. The news that a
sahib, or foreign gentleman, was there, soon spread,
and all that were at home came running to hear what
we had to say. We found an old native sergeant here,
who had retired on his pension, and who was very

kind and civil to us, forcing on us a present of milk, which was most acceptable to my assistant Hanúk."

Beside the above extracts, accounts might have been given of some scenes of a more marked character. Sometimes it has happened that the people seem to be in a perfect *furor* for books, and press upon the missionary greatly. Occasionally scenes of comparative danger are encountered. In what I have chosen to relate I have aimed to present our ordinary work amongst the rural population. To this, I will only add some notes of a journey in the Himmáláyá mountains, to convey, so far as they may do so, some notion of the kind of work to be done there.

"*April 28th.*—Rose early, and climbed the first hill on the road by moonlight. Went to a village a little way from the road, and preached to all the men and boys who were in it, for about half an hour. Forward, and did the same in another village, where we bought some wheat-meal for the people and ourselves. Went on to a third village, and got permission to sit in the shade outside a house. Here we had our breakfast prepared. While waiting for it, the whole village crowded around us, and we talked to them about the gospel a good while.

"The people of these villages seemed very ignorant. They appeared to be afraid of us in some respects. At first they stoutly maintained that they had nothing to sell; but when they saw us begin to pay money for meal, they began to bring it freely from all their houses for sale, and we heard several hand-mills commence operations. We found a man who said that a neighbour, who was absent, could read Hindí, but he would not take a book, which we wished to leave for him. Another man said that his son, who was also absent, could read well; and after some persuasion, he allowed us to leave some tracts for him. But just before night he came to our tent, a distance of at least three and a half miles, and over a most tiresome road, to return the books. He said that Mr. Woodside had told him that he would make inquiry, on his return, whether they had read and understood them, and that the whole village were frightened at the idea of such an inquiry, and were persuaded that if their knowledge did not give satisfaction, they would be punished in some way. We could not persuade him to keep the books. He then made a demand for a few coppers, which he said one of our hill-men had run off without paying. But it happened that both of us saw the money fully and honestly paid. We set out with a rule that everything should be paid in our presence, to avoid disputes of this kind. After he found that the case was going against him, he said that his honesty in bringing back the books, when he found that they could not be used satisfactorily, ought to cause his story to be believed. The fact is, he thought in this way to make us believe his falsehood about the money, and it was this that caused him to take all that trouble, and give up the tracts.

"About noon we left this third village, and went down into the valley of the Jumna. We thought we should have a good deal of shade on the road, but were disappointed; the sun beat upon us with constantly increasing fury, as we left the elevation of the hills. The road was the sharpest descent which I had ever attempted; it turned sharply to the right and left, forming a zig-zag; it was fully three miles down, and so steep that we had to go on foot; the horses slid frequently; I had to plant my foot carefully, in order to prevent a disastrous slide. I reached the river at last, feeling that I had never before exerted myself physically to the same degree. The tent was set up on the bank of the Jumna, and we spent the night there.

"The Jumna, at this place, was a stream about forty feet wide, running very rapidly over a stony

15

bed, probably falling four feet in every hundred. It
presented every appearance of being a raging torrent
thirty feet deep in the rains. There is an iron sus-
pension bridge over it, built by the government.
The hills on both sides are precipitous, leaving only a
narrow patch of bottom land here and there.

"We found a solitary hill-man living here, who
looks after the bridge. We talked to him about
Christ.

"*April 29th.*—A severe morning march up from
the Jumna. In many places the road was too steep
to ride. When our breath was much expended, we
took hold of the horses' tails, and made them assist
us. After ascending, we stopped at a pretty large
village, the name of which I forgot to record. There
was a large two storied temple here, and close to it
a three-storied public building, the lower story of
which was a kind of storehouse for the temple, and
the upper stories empty, and used as sleeping places
for strangers. The temple is one of Siva, containing
only the usual *lingam*. This god, called in the plains
Mahádeo, (the great god,) is here, and wherever we
went in the hills, called Mahású—the last syllable
being, doubtless, a corruption of Shiva, or Siva.
The temple stood in the middle of an oblong court,
with houses on two sides belonging to the temple
establishment, which seemed to be numerous. In
the shade of the temple we had our breakfast cooked,
and our little table set out. There we talked a long
time to the assembled villagers about Christ. Afterward we spent part of the day in the strangers' apartments, talked again to the people, and dined.

"By the side of the large temple was a very small
one, with an image of Kálí, all smeared with the
blood of kids that had been offered to her.

"In the course of this day, an old woman, belonging to the temple, dressed herself up in all her
absurd finery, and offered to dance before us. We

TEMPLES IN INDIA.

gave the people to understand that we did not like to encourage bad women. They told us that in this part of the hills there were no such women; and that though none but bad women dance in the plains, here respectable women do so, before idols and at weddings. However, we still declined to encourage the thing, because they intended the dance to be in honour of the idol; otherwise we would have witnessed it, in order to see as much as possible of their manners and customs.

"A singular exhibition of spiritual vanity and desire of applause to-day. Our coolies made an offering to Mahású, and boasted to us that they had given twelve and a half cents each—a large sum for such a purpose. When we mentioned this to the people of the temple, they replied, with indignation, that all our people together had given *three cents*, and wished for the credit of a large donation. Poor human nature is the same everywhere. After dinner marched again, and talked at another village.

* * * * * * * *

" We had milk and other provisions from the people of this town, and the headman has impressed himself on my memory as the most avaricious man I have ever encountered. After we had paid the full usual price for all that we had obtained through him, and given him a small present for his attentions to us, he began to question us as to how much more money we would have given him had we not given the people books; and offered to gather up and return the books, if we would give him the very smallest sum of money. He complained because we had paid for one article to the man who brought it, saying that it ought to have gone through his hands, in order that he might have secured a part of it. When we expressed some contempt of such extreme cupidity, he said he saw no reason for it; money was the highest good—and 'Oh, how I do love money!' came out with an emphasis and 'unction that would have been the best of all possible reproofs to some close-fisted Christians.

*   *   *   *   *   *   *   *

"Spoke to the few people whom we could find. We happened to touch a small conical stone, which was lying on a large rock near the border of a field, and one of the villagers immediately cried out against us, that we had desecrated his god, and that it would cost him a goat to atone for our transgression. We declined to pay for the goat, and advised him to seek a different object of worship.

"The village near us is named Kachánú. We here found the first apricot and walnut trees.

"*May 3d.*—On the march Mr. Woodside preached in the village called Bandraulí. I was too hoarse to assist him much. In the evening reached a place called Shilaurá, where the same thing occurred.

"During this afternoon's march, we came in sight of the Tauns river. This is one of the tributaries of the Jumna, and quite as large as that river where we crossed it. Our first view of it was gained on rounding the shoulder of a high mountain, when the valley, with a large nice village and a great amount of cultivation, opened upon us through a shower of rain, on which the sun was shining. Our elevation was such that not the faintest murmur of the vexed stream below reached our ears—while we could trace the white foaming torrent for a long distance. Here, as in many places, our road was a narrow cut, from two and a half to five feet in width, in the side of the hill, while there was a clear slope below us, apparently quite down to the river, appearing as if a person once started would roll without remedy a mile and a half to its rocky bed.

*   *   *   *   *   *   *   *

"*May 5th.*—Marched in the morning from Mandhaur to Tikrí. Here we found a village on the top of a ridge, with a temple and very small lodging-house with open sides. Rested part of the day and preached a good deal.

"The architecture of this region is peculiar. The roofs are like the top of a tent: flattish towards the eaves, becoming more steep as they ascend, and ending in sharp points at the top. Around the eaves hangs a fringe of turned wooden pins, fastened loosely on nails, so that they swing in the wind, and rattle against each other. The architecture is decidedly Tátar, or Chinese, rather than Hindú.

"Forward to Píentrá, crossing two small streams, and consequently having a great deal of down and up. Reached the tent late, and dined at near 10, P. M.

"*May 6th.*—Could not leave this beautiful valley without proclaiming the good tidings to the people. and therefore did not march. Mr. Woodside preached, and I was obliged to be nearly silent on account of my throat.

* * * * * * * *

"About 11 o'clock we left this place, and marched to a brook, where we spent a part of the day, and afterward went on to a place called Ohhipál. A large temple, a police station, a shop of sundries, a government dispensary with native doctor, and several ordinary houses, made up the village. The elevation must have been considerable, as the cold was a serious annoyance. We talked to all the people whom we could get together, and left some books. The greater part of the people showed the greatest degree of indifference to our message.

"The road here is much wider than on the other side of the Tauns; but the severity of the ascents and descents is not much less. We had hard work this afternoon. The people have evidently had more intercourse with Europeans, in some respects to their great advantage, and in others not.

15*

"*May 7th.*—Our first halting place was called Patthar Nala—a very pleasant place, but near no village, nor did we pass any on the road. This place is reckoned one of the usual stages; but as the day was Saturday, and we did not wish the Sabbath to be a day of idleness as well as of rest, we marched in the evening to the next village that was near the road, the name of which was Udai. We found our tent pitched near the village. A beautiful water-course brought down a stream for the irrigation of the fields, and a fine orchard of apple and apricot trees was on one of the slopes of the hill. On making inquiry, we learned that the place belonged to the estate of the Ráná of Balsan. Ráná is a title given to small chieftains, though they sometimes have sovereign authority in their territories. The headman of the village sent off information of our arrival to the Ráná, whose residence was at a distance of about a mile and a half. We could not but admire the scenery here. We had passed over a fine wide hill road, latterly along the side of a finely wooded mountain; and our encampment was on one of five ridges, which descended and converged towards a point in a large valley that lay below us. Numerous villages were in sight, and the lower parts of the hills were prettily terraced and cultivated. Here would be a very fine place for a hill mission.

"*May 8th—Sabbath.*—This morning about ten o'clock the Ráná and suite came to see us. We had offered to go and see him first, as a compliment to his rank; but his people would not hear a word of it, saying that the Ráná would think himself disgraced if he failed to pay clergymen the compliment of visiting them first, because he felt that ecclesiastical office placed a man above all worldly rank. The people of the village gathered around us, and I preached about an hour to them, addressing what I said to the Ráná, who assented to it all as good. He then told us something of his history—pointed out, on the top of a neighbouring hill, the ruins of a fort, which had once belonged to the Gurkhas, who had driven him from his territories, and kept possession of them four years. When the Gurkha power was broken by the English, he gathered his people, took and demolished the fort, and handed over his prisoners, three hundred and eighteen in number, to General Ochterlony. The people here have a curious corruption of this general's name—they uniformly call him Lúniákhtar, placing the two first syllables after the two last. The Ráná had evidently been a man of action and energy. His grandson, the heir-apparent, gives small promise of being a worthy successor to him; he is about the dirtiest and most ignorant fellow that we have met in the hills. The old gentleman has a great-grandson, about sixteen years old, a fine boy, whom I wish we could educate. We pleaded with his dirty father to send him to the plains to school, but I fear in vain.

"In the evening we returned the Ráná's visit. Mr. Woodside talked a little while to the people at his house. The house was four stories in height, built on three sides of a court-yard. The lower story seemed to be mostly occupied by the cattle, and the court-yard was full of manure. We returned, on the whole a good deal disgusted at the palace. But though we could not fancy the peculiar kind of civilization seen here, yet justice requires me to say that the Ráná and his people are far in advance of the great body of the hill people. I have no doubt but that he would receive, and treat well, a mission that would include a medical man, a school, &c."

No effort has been made, in selecting matter to represent our experience, to put matters in an encouraging light. The cause of Christ can never be really promoted by deception, by highly colouring facts, nor by concealing what may tend to discourage some persons. For those who support foreign missions on right principles, it is sufficient to know that people are destitute of the gospel and accessible. This, with their knowledge of the promises of God, is enough to cause them to work on with zeal, faith, and patience.

There ought to be much more done in the way of itinerating than is done at present. There is no other way in which the greater part of the people can ever hear the gospel. But the missionaries at present in the field cannot do enough of this work. One man, or perhaps two, at each station, are confined by schools, so that they can only go out during their vacation of one month. Others are bound to their stations by presses and other things, to leave which for any time requires a great deal of management. More than once I have been obliged to have a man constantly going between my tent and the press, when I was out preaching in the country, to carry proofs, business letters, and the like; and had to spend half of the day in work to keep the presses in motion. And it often happens that when we go out, it is to attend a meeting of Synod, or a melá, which it is a shame to neglect; and there is not time on the road to do anything better than to get forward as fast as possible, and preach as much as one can during halts. These things show that there ought to be more missionaries at each station. Superintendents of schools and presses, and others having fixed employments, could then be relieved for a part of each cold season, and all could remain out for about three months, each party at different times, so as to cover the whole season.

If we could have as many men as would be desirable at such a place as Allahabad, a plan might be carried out for thoroughly preaching through that district, which has not yet been done; and it is not wonderful that it has not been done. There are about ten large towns, and five thousand villages and hamlets in it; and at the rate of three a day, which is as great an average of visits as a missionary can pay, it would require over forty years of one man's life—Sundays and holidays included—without one day's rest, or one day's sickness, or one day's attendance at church, or one day's visiting, to preach only once in each of these places. And along with this view of that district, the sad fact ought to be remembered, that it is flanked on both sides by unoccupied districts of greater extent. Almost all the places that we occupy are surrounded by an equally dense population. Large tracts of country lie open on all sides of us; people ready to listen are everywhere; roads to facilitate travel exist in abundance, at least through all the territories of the English, and in some instances, in those of the native princes; and the protection afforded to life and property, and to one peaceably preaching the gospel, is sufficient.

This is a simple, unexaggerated view of the work to be done, and of the facilities for doing it, if only the men were there. I have a hundred times been asked, since I came to America, if we have yet produced any very sensible effect on the country by our labours. In the ninth chapter of this work will be found the answer to this question. But if the Church will look at the field, and our means, she will be surprised to learn that we can give an answer in any respect encouraging. Let the facts stated in this paragraph be pondered. They are highly suggestive.

CHAPTER VII.

THE PREPARATION OF BOOKS FOR THE PRESS.

EVERY missionary who has any leisure for it, and who acquires sufficient skill in the languages used in his field of labour, will desire to do something to bring the power of the press to bear upon the mass of evil around him.   And all have this leisure, who are not particularly engaged in schools, or something as engrossing. If a man's chief work be oral preaching to the heathen, he will generally have all the middle of the day to employ in study of some kind, or in writing and translating, for seven months of the year.   During the other five months, he ought to be in the district, away from the city, and busy in such operations as are described in the last chapter.   But during the seven hot months, he can only go out to preach in the morning and the evening.   A part of the day ought to be used in preparing for such preaching, in thinking how to answer objections, and in talking with the catechist on such matters; but this will still leave him some time. This time he ought to employ in doing such literary work as may most directly aid the object of the preaching.   All missionaries cannot, indeed, be expected to produce anything in this way.   Delicacy of health may prevent.   In many cases, the style formed in learning the language is not sufficiently good for this purpose, though a man may use it effectively in preaching.   The mid-day leisure of many is filled up with the care of schools and presses, and with business connected with the mission.   We are also to remember, that a man will ordinarily be preaching a year or two at least, before he will feel that he has sufficient experience of the ideas and language of the country to write books for the people of it.

All these things make it most necessary that they who have language, leisure, and ability, should use them. A great deal has been done towards securing good translations of the Scriptures; and this object is now so far accomplished, that probably only occasional revisions, for future editions, will be necessary, until the native Hindustání church shall produce scholars of her own, with such learning that they can reproduce the ideas of the Bible correctly, and in an idiom more acceptable to their countrymen than that of foreigners can ever be. Tracts and elementary treatises on religious subjects have been prepared to some extent, the greater part of them having a connection with the controversies between us and the Mohammedans and Hindús. But a great deal more remains to be done: the reading of native Christians is still confined to very few books. Comparative destitution, then, is the first reason why we should all labour in this department if we can. And it must be stated that this destitution is not merely of religious books; we have scarcely any history, philosophy, science or literature, in either dialect of the Hindustání; and what little there is in any of these departments is either Mohammedan or Hindú in its tendency, or mere crude and elementary attempts. Most of it is, therefore, evil in its tendency in various ways; and this is a second reason why we should write for the press. The want of a good literature, using the word in its broadest sense, is one of the greatest hinderances to the work of conversion. And yet if there were nothing extant, which took the place of a literature, it would, in some respects, be better for us; for that which exists misleads the people, and is so thoroughly trusted in, that we can scarcely find any place for the truth. The people have histories, geographies, and various other works; but they are as erroneous as they can be, and the people are as bigoted about them as about their religions. Every one has heard of Hindú astronomy, and how it is connected with mythological and theological fables, till it has become a part of their religion; and the fact that they can calculate eclipses gives the Pandits such credit with the people that it certainly would be better, not merely for the cause of Christianity, but ultimately for science itself, if they knew nothing, and were dependent upon missionaries for the very elements of all knowledge. All have heard of the seven concentric oceans of the Hindús; and it is harder to remove this false idea from the mind, and afterwards implant the truth, than it would be to make a good geographer of a savage. In the matter of history, the Hindús have not a page that is reliable; and yet they have a history, so full of a marvellous antiquity and astonishing deeds and occurrences, that we appear in comparison to be pigmies in exploits and knowledge. The notions of the Mohammedans are just as far from the truth. For instance, if we wish to appeal to history in any way for evidence of the truth of Christianity, they suppose themselves to be in possession of all history already, and will not admit a jot that we can bring forward. They are as completely unbelievers as to Herodotus, Xenophon, Josephus, and all other early historians, as they are of the New Testament. They have received a distorted and fabulous account of the Greeks, and of Alexander, from the Persians; and this they insist on believing, and will have nothing else. All the ecclesiastical history and other writings of the first six centuries after Christ, are to them a perfect nullity; but they suppose that they know all about it. And when we adduce anything of the sort, they say that if there had been any such thing they should have heard of it, and that is the end. And the Hindús have not even so much knowledge of the ancient West—they can scarcely believe that it ever existed. Therefore we have to teach the people not only religion, but also history and science; and we must go back to the very beginnings of knowledge, and clear away the jungle, and plant anew through the whole course. Doubtless we shall secure some native assistance in this; native Christians will help us; but every one will see that for another whole generation foreign assistance will be a necessity.

To enliven this dry chapter, a few amusing instances of the conceit of knowledge will be related. A Pandit once soberly gave me an account of the origin of winds and storms. I do not think that all Pandits are as ignorant as he was; and yet his *extravaganza* may be taken as a specimen of a thousand prevailing ideas. He said—There is a great monster, that lives near the outer verge of the first circle of ocean, that is, the salt water ocean. He is several thousand miles long. He was one of the gods, but for some offence has been confined in that lonely situation. He lies near the surface of the water, with his face above it, and turns about continually. His motions cause the continual heaving of the ocean; his respirations cause the tides; his breath, discharged in various directions, cause the ordinary winds; and when the water occasionally dashes in his face, and incommodes his nostrils, he blows the water out of his nose with an impatient snort, which causes a storm, that proceeds to the utmost bound of the earth in the direction in which he may happen to be lying. Storms in other directions are the *reflections* of such storms as strike against Mount Sumeru.

In a discussion with a Musalmán I brought forward the idea that in Christian countries art, learning and morals are in a better condition than in any other. He denied our superiority in general terms; and said that, as to art, it was essentially idolatrous, and Musalmáns could not practise it; but if they would, it was well known that their fancy, imagination and taste

16

were much greater than those of Europeans; as to
learning, we were no match for them: rhetoric we
evidently could make very little of, while they had it
in perfection; and so they had logic, of which Europeans had not the first rudimental idea—had not even
a name for it; and their philosophy accounted for
everything in heaven and in earth, *and for much that
was in other places*, while it was perfectly certain that
Europeans had no notion of spiritual and abstract
ideas. He would, indeed, acknowledge that we had
a greater acquaintance with steam, and with the
science of mechanics generally, than they had; but
this was a low kind of knowledge, to possess which
showed no grandeur of ideas, no cultivation of intellect, no taste, nor anything but a qualification for
being what we are, the mechanics of the world! He
said that this knowledge was only a refinement of
brute force, by which we held in subjection a great
part of the world, not to our honour, but to the exposure of our grossness. Morals he gave up to us,
saying with a wicked wink, that rustics and low persons were usually found to be more correct in some
respects than gentlemen.

Two standing objections, which Musalmáns make
to any proof drawn from the New Testament are,
that Christians have corrupted it, cutting out and
inserting what they pleased; and that when the
Mohammedan army took Alexandria and burned the
library, every copy of the New Testament was lost.
Now a correct knowledge of geography and history
proves that neither of these things could have happened. I have often had occasion to show this to
visitors and others in discussion; but those that are
educated in the native fashion, deny every fact and
statement which we can bring forward bearing on
these points; and, before we can prove anything relating to them, we must go back and prove a thousand
subsidiary matters, historical and geographical. In

short, the whole foundation of reasoning with them on such matters must be laid *ab initio*. Once a native friend of mine, who had been pretty well educated in English in a government school, made these objections; and I appealed to him whether he did not *know* that they could not stand. He answered that he knew it very well; but, said he, "what will you, or what can I do with learned Musalmáns, who have only been taught on the native system? I have stated the matter to them; and they answer me that I am deceived by a systematic manufacture of geography and history to answer Christian purposes; and that the government, professing to be neutral as to religion, is really in secret helping the missionairies, by using books of falsehood in its schools." Ignorance of this kind is more invincible than mere absence of knowledge; and to deal with people so stuffed with false notions, and so confident in them, requires the exercise of the greatest talent and industry.

An account of a Mohammedan map of the world, lately published at Lucknow, which claims to be the Athens, as it certainly is the Paris of the Musalmáns of India, will illustrate the matter here spoken of. The author has partly got up to the European idea that the earth is round; but he takes it to be a circular plane. His map of the *whole* world is therefore shaped like *one hemisphere* of our maps. Instead of dividing it into zones equally each side of the equator, he has adopted their old idea of seven climates all north of the equator, which he has put far south of its true place. As to the countries of Asia, their relative positions are not ludicrously wrong; but most of the countries of Europe are small islands northwest of Asia. One of these islands is gravely called Europe, another England, another London; another, a very small one, Spain; and another, three times as large as that called Spain, is named Andalusia! America is nowhere; but one of its towns is on the western coast of Africa.

These things are enough to show that missionaries and other Europeans have a science and literature to create for India; except so far as East Indians and native Christians may be enlisted in this great work. I might show this further if I would go into an examination of their poetry and works of fiction, and display their corrupt character; but that can easily be imagined, and it would not be decent to write about it. Government school teachers will aid in this work materially; but as they have very little to do with teaching Christianity, their efforts will tend to pull down the edifice of falsehood, more than to build up religious truth.

Our missions have not been backward in helping in this branch of the work. The reader will remember the statement that the Rev. James Wilson furnished several of our first tracts at Allahabad. He also did the greater part of the work of preparing notes on the Korán, which we published in the Roman character. The translation in Urdú is by a Mohammedan, made for their own purposes. The notes are intended to furnish missionaries and catechists with arguments in controversy. Our friend E. G. Fraser, Esq. furnished Mr. Wilson with the materials for a great part of the notes; and he wrought them into form, and added to them. My part of the work was an occasional suggestion and clipping of redundancies, and making the indices. Mr. Wilson also assisted in getting out the first complete edition of the Urdú Old Testament, called that of Messrs. Shurman and Hawkins.

A volume of sermons in Urdú, for the native Christians, was projected, collected and published by our mission. Its authors were numerous, including most of our missionaries, who were then in the country.

The first Bible in Hindí was a translation from the English. When the work began to be out of print, the North India Bible Society took measures to have it thoroughly revised. Mr. Owen of our mission was appointed editor of the work. There were others on the translation committee, of whom I was one; but the business was almost all done by Mr. Owen. My share of it was a few suggestions as to certain passages, and the commencement of the printing of it. In this book, ornamental and large letters are used in the beginning of the chapters, the first work in the Nágarí letter that has been printed in this manner.

The Urdú Bible was soon expended, and a new edition needed. It was generally agreed that it required some revision. The late Rev. J. A. Shurman, of Benares, was requested to revise it, assisted by me. His valuable life was cut short when the Old Testament was about half done; and I finished it, with such assistance as I could get—not attempting so close a revision, however, as the first part had received. It is not probable that the translation is yet quite as good as it ought to be, and we may look for further improvements. The New Testament revision was in the hands of a separate committee.

The Lodiana Mission, assisted by the late Rev. W. Bowley, of the English Church Missionary Society, published a book of Psalms and Hymns at our press at Allahabad. That edition has been used up, and several of our missionaries were lately engaged in revising and greatly improving the work for republication.

The same mission has produced a large number of tracts and books. Their most considerable works are, the greater part of the New Testament, and the Psalms, in the Panjábí language, and a large dictionary and a grammar of that language.

I cannot fully detail the work done by our missions,

16*

through the presses. My own part of it, beside that
mentioned above, has been as follows : 1. Eight original lectures on the eighth chapter of Proverbs. 2. A
translation (with additions) of the American Tract
Society's tract on the New Birth. 3. A translation
of Gallaudet's Ruth. 4. A translation of Watts and
Henry on Prayer, as prepared by Dr. Bouton, of
Concord, N. H., with an original introductory lecture.
5. A translation of the Dairyman's Daughter; and,
6, of the Young Cottager. 7. A translation of Flavel's
Fountain of Life. 8. A translation of Dr. Hodge's
Way of Life.

My connection with the press also caused me a great
deal of labour in looking over other people's books, and
preparing their copy for the press. This, and the part
that I took in the translation of our Confession of
Faith and Catechisms, probably amounted to half as
much labour as the translation of the works above
named. The subject of job-work, and of work and
assistance rendered to me by my catechist, has been
mentioned in the third and fourth chapters.

A peculiar kind of perplexity is felt by all who attempt translation into an oriental language, more than
by those who are rendering one European language
into another. I have no other reason for mentioning
this here, than that it illustrates the state of mind and
opinion on certain subjects, amongst both Mohammedans and Hindús. This perplexity arises from the
fact that words meaning, or rather appearing to mean,
the same as some English word, do not convey the
same idea to a native mind that they do to ours. We
need to go back of the dictionary, and find out of
what the idea in question is composed, in a native's
mind. For example, the word *gunáh* in Urdú, and
páp in Hindí, mean *sin*. But if we were to ask either
Musalmán or Hindú, What is sin? he would define it
very differently from what we should do. The Musalmán would consider touching a dog as real, though

perhaps not so great, a sin as killing a man. He
would think it as offensive to God, if not so mischievous otherwise. His conscience would condemn
him as readily for mistake in the forms of prayer, as
for not praying at all; and for breaking a fast, as for
picking a pocket, especially if it were the pocket of an
unbeliever. A Hindú would consider his spittle falling
on his person to be sin, and probably would not in the
least be troubled by lying and cheating; because an
outward defilement interdicts religious services and
eating with his caste, while acts that we call sinful do
no such thing. *Nayá janam*, or *nai paidáish*, means
the *new birth;* but a Hindú left to himself would suppose these terms to mean the transmigration of the
soul into another body, in which to be born the second
time. A Musalmán would certainly ask Nicodemus's
question about it. *Pákízagí* and *pabitrtá* mean purity
or holiness. But a Musalmán thinks holiness is being
washed with water; and a Hindú thinks it to be the
same, or to be marked with ashes, mud from the
Ganges, or cowdung, or to possess a certain kind of
stone, or to live at Benares, or to see the Ganges, or
any one of a thousand more things. *Páki* is only
another form of *pákízagí*, and ought also to mean holiness; but colloquially it is applied to shaving off all
the hairs of the body, save those on the head. These
statements have been suggested to me by the recol-
lection that our mission once published a list of theological terms in English and Hindustání, in the hope
of aiding to settle some vexed questions amongst missionaries.

No more appropriate close of this chapter can be
found than the questions — Ought the Church to
grudge her best men to such a work as the formation
of the literature of the thirty millions of Upper India?
And it is not for this thirty millions only: their language is more or less known all over India, and their
literature always has influenced, and always will in-

fluence, that of various other dialects and languages of Central and Southern India. North India is the home of all the great races of the country, and the source of all the great influences that have spread over the whole land. Ought her very best men, who have taste and talent for teaching by the college or the press, to wish for a better field than one where so much is to be done? Can her finest linguists find a better field than the one here described? I take it for granted that these questions address men who do not ask, Where can we live easiest and gain most honour—where can we get most worldly good? But, Where can we do most for Christ, and for the advancement of the highest human interests? Certain it is, we do not want in the mission field men of any other spirit. But ought a dull scholar to be sent to combat with the subtleties of an elaborate and skilful false philosophy? Ought one without fluency or address to be considered "good enough for a missionary" to a people polished, accomplished, quick, subtle, fluent and conceited? Ought the Church to keep a man at home because he is a man of talent—or the man himself to object to "bury himself in the obscurity of a mission field?" My sober conviction, after seventeen years' experience and observation, is, that until the Church is more ready to send out her first-rate men, and more of such men are willing to go, to the foreign missions, she will not have done her duty, nor will her missions prosper as she expects, nor will she at home avoid the evils attendant upon "withholding more than is meet."

CHAPTER VIII.

RELATIONS WITH EUROPEANS AND EAST INDIANS, AND THEIR
INFLUENCE ON OUR WORK.

THE subject of this chapter is not very directly connected with my own doings as a missionary; but it is
intimately so with my experience;—and a full view of
what a missionary has to do in India, and of his com-
forts, his aids, and his discouragements—in a word, of
his *life*—cannot be given without an account of his
connections with society.

In America, every man of good education, tolerable manners, and decent dress, is considered a gentleman. It is not so in English society. Amongst the
English in India, connection and profession are the
paramount distinctions. A commissioned officer is a
gentleman; so is a covenanted civilian; so are their
sons, though they may not succeed in getting into
either of these professions, and have to put up with
some subordinate appointment; so are any persons
who may be known to be connected with the upper,
or upper-middle classes of England, though in subordinate places; so are medical men and chaplains.
Missionaries, on account of their education, but mainly
because of their ordination, are admitted to this society. If there is ever any reserve in admitting
them, the reason of it is to be found in the fact that
many early English missionaries were men of small
education; and it has happened that some persons of
very low origin and education have been admitted to
the office in India, and some societies and individuals
have sent out as missionaries persons who were not
qualified to mix in society; and thus the social position
of a missionary has been rendered somewhat doubtful,
at least to some people, who are fastidious. Some few
East Indians, connected with society by a mixed but

legitimate parentage, and some illegitimate offspring of very great men, are admitted; but the great body of that people are considered to be out of it. A merchant, who buys articles for exportation, is a gentleman; but if the same man keep a shop for selling anything by retail, he is not a gentleman. There is no great fault to be found with these distinctions, except that they are a little too unbending: some persons retain their places in society by their connections, who are unfit for it; and some, from want of connections, are excluded when qualified to do honour to it. Natives of rank are sometimes found in public parties, but rarely have much to do with European society.

It is the custom in India for the new comer to a station to call on the residents with whom he would like to be acquainted. Unless it be ascertained that the person so calling has no claim to the society which he thus seeks to be admitted to, the residents return his call; and if he be a married man, the ladies go to see his wife. If they are persons of sufficient standing, invitations to dinner are given by those who return the call; but this is not obligatory. A missionary may thus call on whom he pleases, and very few will be rude enough to neglect to return the civility. After this, people of a quiet turn, and the decidedly religious, invite them to their houses occasionally; but the more gay and worldly treat them with only civility. But when the missionary family is settled in a place for a considerable time, and the English residents are changed, the circle of their acquaintance may become much more restricted; for the new comers may not be devout enough to wish for the acquaintance of religious people, and therefore will not call on them, while the missionary is thus given to understand that he may keep his distance. Casually he may become known to them, but generally a large part of the residents of the same station will

remain strangers to him. At a small station this will
not be the case so much as at a larger one: the minor
stations contain so few people, that there is both more
need of the mission family in society, and more time
to attend to them; while at the larger places they are
of less consequence to other people, and various public amusements and parties take up people's time sufficiently to combat a faint wish to cultivate the missionary's acquaintance, if it were in existence.

The high officers of government acknowledge our
standing by occasionally inviting us to dinner. The
Governor General, the Commander-in-chief of the
army, and the Lieutenant-Governor of the Northwest
Provinces, have done this repeatedly.

At the same time that we have, in this way, a
standing with the highest, we are not excluded from
the acquaintance of those who are "not in society."
Most missionaries freely visit respectable persons
who are not recognized as having any rank, and some
of our most valued friends are amongst them. In
associating with them we very probably sometimes
incur the scorn, or pity, or contempt of some who are
"in society," and may forfeit some civilities from
them. I have experienced something of this; but
never had any doubt about which class I could most
influence for good, and therefore never hesitated to
do what some people would call descending. However, it is generally practically acknowledged, that we
may go where we please without losing caste.

At the larger stations it is sometimes quite a task
to call on all the older residents. I never attempted
it. And this operates to hinder some persons from
making the acquaintance of missionaries. And some
new comers at a station probably find out who are the
covenanted civil officers, and the officers of the military force, and call on them without thinking to inquire whether there are others who may be entitled
to such a civility. I have known some persons, who

had lived six months at a station before they found out that that there were any missionaries there; and then felt delicate about calling at so late a day. Others stayed away altogether, from want of interest in missions; and when asked, at other stations, if they had known the missionaries, and anything about their work, answered, in substance, "No; I hardly ever heard of them, and saw nothing of their work. I suppose they do very little beside living well and taking it easy." No doubt these people are often quite honest in saying such things, except so far as they are culpable for not taking pains to see what was being done.

There certainly were many persons at Allahabad and Agra, during my residence at those places, who could not have known what the mission was doing; for they never visited the press or the schools, and probably never asked anybody whether there were such things. They never encountered any native Christians; for none of them were engaged in business that brought them into contact with Europeans outside of the mission. They never, or rarely, could see us at our preaching places, because they rode on the high roads outside of the city, and avoided the places where the natives mostly congregate, on account of the various unpleasant things that assail the senses there—and these were the very places where some of us could have been seen frequently. A gentleman residing in a country house outside of New York, never going to church when he can avoid it, never seeing a religious periodical, avoiding all religious society, and never making any inquiries whatever as to religious people or movements, and, moreover, being much predisposed to look on all such with dislike, may easily come to believe and say, (and such people *do* say,) that the American Bible Society does no real work, and uses its funds corruptly. Such a gentleman would be a fair parallel to many who have lived in India, and have done missions a mischief, because it was supposed that they must know all about them from having been on the spot. I have known two American travellers to move together through the provinces we occupy, and never come near one of our places, though at the same stations; and at the same time that they were making themselves ridiculous there by reporting the Unitarian to be the largest and leading denomination in America, they were, as many Americans will naturally believe, qualifying themselves to report on our missions. Another, and much more distinguished traveller, being a man of a gentlemanly *mind* as well as *station*, though not agreeing with us in religious opinion, came to us as a fellow-countryman ought to do, looked at our work and made himself able to report it fairly, so far as his own theological system allowed him to see it in the right light, gave us a great pleasure by making use of us, and got some of his best information for his letters from us. But there are few like him. A hundred intelligent young men may easily be found, who have each spent five years in India, whose combined knowledge of it is not equal to that gathered by him in a few weeks. Many pay no attention to anything but their regiments and their amusements.

But there are almost always a few truly devout and religious persons at every station, who kindly take notice of the missionaries, and encourage them in their work. His heart must be insensible indeed, who fails to feel great gratitude for the comfort derived from such society and such help, and the most sincere friendship to such persons. It would, of course, be invidious to name such friends, and they would not desire it; but it is necessary to acknowledge their kindness at least in general terms. And the English community in India, considered as a whole, is an exceedingly liberal one, both in feeling, and in pecuniary aid to missionary efforts. Their liberality as to money

17

will appear from what will be stated hereafter. Their
kind feeling and true charity towards those who are of
different denominations, deserves special notice here.
There are very few indeed who look superciliously
upon dissenters; and no regular missionary is without
help in supporting his schools, building his chapels,
and carrying on any of his operations that may require extra outlay. Presbyterian missions sometimes
meet with a degree of special favour, as not being
English dissenters; but the difference made is not
great, nor often perceived. As a matter of course the
missions of the English Church are better supported
than any others; and they ought to be so by their
own people. Their missionaries are more noticed in
society, as is but natural too; but other missionaries
cannot complain of any want of kindness, or of any
tendency to hand them over to "uncovenanted mer-
cies." Where there are many men, there will be
some weak and bigoted men; and we have now and
then encountered one who evidently thought us an
evil—perhaps a chaplain, who spoke of us contemptu-
ously, or tried to keep his people from aiding us; but
such men have had bad success, and always injured
themselves by anything like active hostility. Episcopal missionaries journey and preach with us to the
heathen, notwithstanding the silly law, by which the
English Church has excommunicated herself from all
the rest of Christendom, by denying ministerial communion to all out of her own pale. Some of my oldest
and dearest friends are of their number.

The benefit of the association of missionaries with
English society is not confined to the missionaries.
There have been many cases of conversion, resulting
from their labours, both amongst Englishmen of all
grades, and the East Indians. Many anecdotes might
be told to show that the benefits of missions are not
confined to the natives. The Presbyterian Church at
Agra, and four large European and East Indian con-

gregations at Calcutta, are the fruit of missionary labour. Numerous individuals have been brought to the knowledge of the truth, who have afterward been very useful to the various missions in the country. Our own missions have been useful in this respect; and it would give me a great deal of pleasure to record instances of this kind, did not delicacy forbid.

Formerly the chaplains on the East India Company's establishment were generally worldly men; too often a discredit to Christianity, and a snare to their people. They are appointed by the Court of Directors in such a way that the appointments are virtually made by single individuals; and if a director has a nephew or friend in orders, whose circumstances make such an appointment desirable, he puts him on the Company's establishment, sometimes without any regard to his character or habits; and thus it happens that some of the chaplains still are, and almost all of them used to be, as utterly without religion as any person in decent society can be. And it is easier to convict a man of felony in a criminal court, than to get rid of a clergyman who is a disgrace to his profession. When, after the revival of religion commenced in England, and, through the exertions of Dr. Buchanan and one or two pious directors, a few pious chaplains were sent out, the great change commenced. The Baptist Mission at Serampore was flourishing at that time, and there began to be some Englishmen in India, who had not, as the proverbial expression went, thrown their baptism overboard when passing the Cape of Good Hope. Then missionaries were sent into various parts of the country; and their devout and correct deportment made it no longer possible for a drunken or wicked chaplain to hold up his head in society, unless he were a man of extraordinary effrontery. Pious gentlemen and ladies, whose piety was often the fruit of missionary labour, also influenced the chaplains favourably. As soon as religion began to take the place of impiety in this way, the effect of it extended in some measure to the Court of Directors; and many gentlemen amongst them have conscientiously used their power of nominating chaplains, so that now many of them are truly worthy men, in many cases aiding missions as much as they can, and some performing in a manner the work of missionaries themselves. The great majority of the chaplains, indeed, do credit to the religion they profess; though, a large number of the most exemplary being Tractarians, there are comparatively few willing to be seen countenancing the missions of any other Church than their own.

The present venerable Bishop of Calcutta, and his Archdeacon, are men of the right sort. They have not hesitated to visit our schools, to encourage us, to recommend our operations to the notice and help of their people, and to take our part in conversations with their own Tractarian clergymen. But though they do all this in passing through the country, as did also the present Bishop of Madras, Dr. Dealtry, when Archdeacon of Calcutta, yet when they come to publish the account of their tours, they are obliged to follow the policy of a State Church, and see nobody in the field but themselves. From their accounts, one would never dream that they had kindly visited our schools, or even heard of them. But if the exigencies of their official position prevent them from telling that they did so truly a Christian thing as to encourage and treat kindly Presbyterians, my position, happily, allows me to acknowledge their kindness with gratitude and thanks.

Bishop Wilson has always treated us personally with great kindness. He caused all our mission to be invited to meet him at a large dinner party at Allahabad. My wife cherishes a volume of his sermons, which he gave her, with his autograph on the title-page; and he prayed publicly for our mission by name at this party, and named it in a sermon in the church. The Bishop is most affable. At a breakfast, where I met him, I blundered into a discussion with him concerning the proper interpretation of a verse in the New Testament. When he found that his own clergymen, who were present, agreed with me, and that the commentaries gave him no support, he gave up with perfect good nature, showing no disposition to resent, or to stand upon his official dignity. He is accustomed to pray for guests, and any friends in special danger or affliction, by name. When I was last in Calcutta, he invited me to one of his public breakfasts, and at morning worship named me, prayed for our church, "for all the churches in that great country from which he comes, and finally for all the family of Protestant churches throughout the world." A great many anecdotes of his eccentric manners are afloat in India; but I will not repeat them. These are sufficient to illustrate, so far, our position and relations to the Episcopal Church in India.

From what has been said it will easily be gathered, that the state of religion is better now than formerly in the nominally Christian community in India; and this is true. I do not know that there has been much change for the better amongst the purely European part of the population in the last fifteen years, nor has there been any deterioration; but there has been a great improvement in the East Indian class: there are a great many more of them now than then, who take a part in religious movements. For further information as to this class of persons, I must refer the reader to the article especially relating to them in in this volume.

Various intimations of having received pecuniary aid in India, for several of our schemes, have been given. It will be gratifying to the friends of missions in America to hear to what extent, and how opportunely, the help of the English community has been given to us; and therefore I will mention, somewhat in detail, the matters in which they have aided

17*

us within my experience.   All our missions have had similar experience.

In speaking, in the fifth chapter, of the way in which the mission church and one of the chapels at Allahabad were built, I have already acknowledged important assistance.

In addition to the account already given of the Presbyterian church at Agra, the following statement is made to exhibit the influence of Europeans and East Indians on our work.   The members of this church, after arriving at Agra, and finding themselves without a minister or place of meeting, formed an alliance with an open communion Baptist church. They attended the services there, and assisted in paying the pastor.   Not long after this arrangement was entered upon, Mr. Wilson from Allahabad and Mr. Rankin from Futtehgurh, were sent to Agra to form a new station of our missions there.   They had every thing to begin anew.   For this reason they were induced to join the alliance with the Baptists; at first it was certainly understood that the Presbyterians were to enjoy equal privileges with the original congregation; at least, the Presbyterians thought it was so understood.   But soon our people learned that they were not to be allowed to baptize a child in the chapel, though it was ostentatiously called "The Union Chapel," and the immersionists had a cistern in it, and administered baptism in their own way there. The Presbyterians did not complain of this, for they were willing to accord some kind of precedence to those who had first occupied the place.   The other party, however, seemed to be hurt by our friends' baptizing the child at all while in connection with them, though it was done in a private house; and they seemed determined, therefore, to crush out the last appearances of Presbyterianism at once.   Accordingly when the Presbyterian part of this curiously constructed church had received a new member, and wished to ordain him as a Ruling Elder, and one of the original Allahabad members had consented to be ordained as Deacon, they refused to allow a special service to be held in the chapel for this purpose. They could have had no other good reason for refusing than that which is here supposed. It was manifestly to their injury to do so. They probably thought they could prevent our further organization; and they were permitted by Providence to try to do it, in order that it might lead the Presbyterians to separate from them, and exert themselves to build up a church according to their own consciences, without any undue compliances; at any rate this was the result. Messrs. Wilson and Rankin commenced services in a private room; and when the new mission-house was finished, the service was held in that until the end of November, 1851. Mr. Rankin was soon obliged to leave the station, and finally the country, by ill-health, after which Mr. Wilson continued to be pastor till he also left Agra for America in the latter part of 1850. I was at Agra on a visit, which was connected with a preaching tour, a little while before Mr. Wilson left, and he and I pressed the wants of the place so upon the notice of the Rev. Mr. Scott, who went out to India with me, and was then at Futtehgurh, that he consented to occupy it for a year, if I would then relieve him, if possible. There was another special reason for our keeping some one at Agra, besides considerations connected with this congregation, which will appear in a future paragraph. Mr. Scott remained a year, and preached to this people amongst other engagements; when I succeeded him in the same for a year and a half. I was followed in the pastoral charge by a minister of the Free Church of Scotland, the Rev. Thomas Grieve Clark. Mr. Clark did not remain long. He accepted a call to a Free church in Bombay. It was a disagreeable thing to be obliged to transfer this church to other hands; but as it did not result in any rupture of most friendly relations, and as the church has amicably come back to us, the subject need only to be thus referred to, amongst the things that have a bearing on our relations in India.

This church has built for itself a very pretty, though very singular edifice, at a cost of about six thousand dollars. It is well placed for the civil station, but fully three miles from the military. The members of this church, when they began to build, gave each a month's income, except in the case of ladies whose husbands did not belong to our body. One such lady, however, paid for the steeple and pulpit, as special donations. The remainder of the money was chiefly raised by a subscription amongst the English community at that and other stations; but there were various little matters, in the finishing and fitting up of the place, that caused several supplementary subscriptions, which bore heavily on the members, and were met with a very good spirit. This was a great undertaking for so small a church, and the aid they received from the public was very liberal. The property vests in the church, not in the mission. The new building was dedicated on the first Sabbath of December, 1851, after my arrival at the place, and just before Mr. Scott's departure. Several new members were admitted on this occasion.

Several gentlemen not connected with any mission have contributed handsomely to the printing of works in behalf of Christianity. I have not space to attempt an enumeration of these works, though I notice the subject as a most interesting one. Some have written tracts, and procured their publication. The desire to use the press is sure to grow up in a cultivated community; and therefore the connection between missions and the Europeans and East Indians is likely, in this respect, to be of still more importance in future.

A Tract and Book Society existed for some time at Benares, and received a considerable amount in contributions from Europeans; but, its support after a time falling off, its action has ceased for some years past. Our press once had an alliance with this Society, so that its publications were put on the American Tract Society's list, and the number that one society alone could have printed was thus doubled. A Tract Society has for some time been pretty well supported by the English community at Agra, and is publishing a valuable series of tracts for the natives. It also keeps a depot of English religious books, for the supply of residents in North India, which is a very useful part of its operations. A Bible Society was formed at Agra when Mr. Wilson first went there, and he was chosen its Secretary; and those of us, who have filled his place in the mission, have been its Secretaries ever since. The connection, which it was desirable that we should maintain with these Societies, has at all times been one of our reasons for retaining Agra as a station. In addition to these great societies, which are intended for the whole North-west Provinces, there is a Protestant Association at Agra, intended to meet the efforts of the Papists, who have made that place the seat of a Bishopric. This association has published some lectures which I delivered at Agra, called out by the aggressive movements of the Papists; and will further exert itself to supply the community with such books and tracts as may be an antidote to the poison sowed by them.

A female day-school at Allahabad is a very good example of many similar operations, which are supported by the European community. It was established, superintended, and supported by subscriptions gathered, by several ladies in succession, till at last its superintendence was handed over to our mission. It is still doing its part towards introducing female

education into India. This school was got up and
maintained by ladies of the first rank in society; and
a very similar one is taught, and mostly supported, at
Agra, by one of the most humble of East Indian
women. We thus see how the cause of truth is aided
equally by persons at either end of the social scale.
At all our stations we receive valuable aid from the
English to support our high and vernacular schools.
Some schools at out stations are entirely sustained by
them. There is no doubt but that several more able
and trustworthy native Christian teachers than we
have at our disposal would be cheerfully supported in
various places by the friends residing there. I have
had a great deal to do in collecting these subscriptions, and know that their amount could at any time
have been increased, had circumstances demanded it.

Our schools at Agra are in a special manner connected with the European and East Indian community,
both by their origin and their object. As it is desirable that our plans as to these schools should be well
known, I shall not hesitate to give a rather full
account of them; and to do so it will be necessary to
go back and give some intimations of what preceded
them.

When all the government offices had been concen-
trated at Agra, the European and East Indian population became very large. Amongst Protestants
there was only one school of even respectable character for the poorer English and East Indians; and the
terms of that were so high, that comparatively few
could avail themselves of it. It was kept by an East
Indian Baptist minister, who had formerly been a
missionary in connection with the Serampore mission.
He was a very good man, and not a poor scholar; but
still he and his wife were no match for the Popish
priests and nuns, who had set up boys' and girls'
schools there, and were likely to do Protestantism no
small harm. This gentleman being a Baptist, and his

school private property, having no public body to
guaranty either its efficiency or its permanence, prevented the Christian public from aiding it, so as to
cheapen it and render it more efficient. Though the
community would fully allow that Baptists are true
Christians, they very naturally objected to their children being educated where they would be very likely
to contract a prejudice against the views of their
parents, on so important a matter as baptism. But
this consideration had less weight there than the
necessity of some cheaper and more efficient school,
to educate Protestant youth, and to counteract the
manifest schemes of the Papists. Therefore several
leading gentlemen in the government service took up
the matter, contributed a large sum of money, appointed a committee of management, bought one house
and hired another, engaged an Episcopal clergyman
and his wife as principals, and established *The Protestant Academy* in male and female departments.
Our Mr. Wilson was one of the committee, and one of
our ruling elders was the committee's secretary. The
Baptist minister, whose school was injured by the new
one, was appointed one of its teachers. Thus a strong
effort was made to unite all kinds of Protestants in its
support. By great exertions a large number of pupils
were collected, and all went on well at first. But
there were two fatal defects in the plan:—it was not
possible to make the tuition fees low enough to secure
the original design; and its prosperity depended on a
single life, or the health of a single man. The principal belonged to no body of men who could always
supply his place when needful. After a short time
the principal became ill, and was obliged to resign his
appointment. His place was supplied, on the recom-
mendation of some good people in Calcutta, by a man
whom the bishop ordained for the purpose—supposed
to be a very good man, and therefore thought, by
those who recommended him, to be fit for *anything*

up the country. But he proved to be without talent, skill or learning. Under him the institution died a death so sudden, that it was clearly proved to have had no stamina before. The Baptist minister, even while the servant of the institution, issued private circulars giving notice to parents that he would re-establish his school, seceded with a number of the pupils, and contributed to the ruin of the academy. The committee were soon left without teachers or scholars, and with a debt amounting to considerably more than the property in hand.

Soon after the failure of this institution its friends, especially the late Mr. Thomason, Lieutenant-Governor, began to wish that our mission would undertake its revival. They represented to Mr. Wilson, that it could succeed only as a mission-school; and that there was no other mission but ours able to undertake it. Mr. Wilson had had such thoughts before, and now began to lay plans for the undertaking. He advocated the renewal, in some shape, of the Protestant Academy, and spoke of his hopes of a Theological Seminary, to grow out of it eventually. The want of men, and the want of a precedent for precisely such a mission-school, led to postponement, and Mr. Wilson was obliged to return home before anything was done; but he left the scheme as a kind of legacy to his successors. After Mr. Scott took his place, he too began to advocate the plan. With the help of the Secretary to the late academy he wrote and printed a pamphlet on the subject, which was circulated amongst all our missionaries in India, and secured their almost unanimous approval of the scheme. He was thus encouraged to send the plan to our Executive Committee.

When the matter was thus laid before the Executive Committee, they approved the scheme, and requested Mr. Fullerton to leave Mynporie and commence the boys' school. They also expressed an intention to send out another man to aid him. This order reached us at the close of 1851, shortly after my arrival at Agra. As the Committee intimated a desire that a commencement should be made during that cold season, Mr. Fullerton removed his family in February, and the school was opened on the 2d of March, 1852. We began it in a small hired bungalow, near the Presbyterian church, with six scholars.

Although I was not expected to take any part in the instruction of the school, yet Mr. Fullerton insisted that I should take upon myself the greater part of the arrangements to be made for it. With his help, therefore, and with the advice of several friends, I published a small pamphlet as an advertisement. In this we announced the principles, plan, and arrangements for the school, and made an appeal to the public. According to this plan the tuition fees were made about half the amount that had been usually paid in private schools. This at once brought the school within reach of a great number of people, who could not previously pay for schooling; and it encouraged benevolent persons to pay the fees for occasional very poor children. This was the operation of our plan that we had anticipated; and it makes our school in a measure a great public charity. When I was leaving India the matter of rendering aid to poor scholars, both in the boys' and girls' schools, was being systematized, and placed in charge of a committee of persons desirous of doing good. The number of children of both sexes already receiving assistance was considerable.

We found ourselves peculiarly situated as to a place in which to keep this school. We had been authorized to hire a house for Mr. Fullerton's family, and must, of course, have some place for the school; but whether we should hire one house large enough for both purposes, or a small one for each, the expense

would be considerable.   We had no resources for buying a place save the sum appropriated for the rent of
a dwelling-house a year, and the contribution that the
Presbyterian church gave for my services.   This we
could appropriate to any local object without reference to the Executive Committee in New York, under
their own rule about local contributions.   The sum
was not then definitely settled, but the church proposed to give me one thousand rupees at once, to enable me to buy a place.   As the sum that would be
saved by having no rent to pay, and this one thousand
rupees, would be a considerable part of the sum necessary for purchasing a house, we were greatly inclined
to make further efforts.   Mr. Fullerton had not yet
arrived, and left all the matter to my decision.   I
was afraid to undertake to raise so large a sum as
would be necessary to complete the undertaking; but
Mrs. Warren urged and encouraged a series of efforts,
that resulted in the most complete success.   This was
neither the first nor the last time when my wife was
the suggester, encourager and promoter of my most
successful efforts.   Other friends also, in this case, advised me to go forward.   I called on Mr. Thomason,
the Lieutenant-Governor, and asked his advice about
the advertising pamphlet, and his aid to our scheme.
He gave several suggestions, and a thousand rupees.
After this I secured the assistance of the leading
civilians at Agra, several of whom gave me two hundred rupees each.   Several kind friends gave me their
names as sureties at a bank, so that I might at once
have command of the necessary funds until the sub-
scribers should find it convenient to pay.   As soon as
this was arranged we completed the purchase of a
large house, out of repair, but in a very good situation.   It was built for a lyceum, ball-room, and Ma-
sonic hall; and therefore had large rooms, and was
quite the kind of place required for the school.   We
put it into a thorough state of repair, and so divided

it that Mr. Fullerton's family and the school had in it quite sufficient apartments. We did not then expect the school to increase to such an extent as to make the house too small for the family, under two or three years at least; and we saw that when it should do so, it would still leave two good rooms for an assistant, or that could be applied to any other useful purpose. When the school had been kept for two months in the small hired bungalow, it was removed to the new place; and in one month more Mr. and Mrs. Fullerton were settled in it. The account at the bank was settled and closed up by the end of that year, and the house was paid for without any appropriation having been made for it by the Executive Committee, except the amount that would have been paid by that time for the rent of Mr. Fullerton's house. The school increased so much beyond our expectations, by the beginning of 1853, that the house became too small for a family; yet it afforded sufficient rooms for Mr. Williams, who joined our mission from America about that time, and was unmarried. This building cost about five thousand and five hundred rupees.

The Rev. R. E. Williams was an old friend of Mr. Fullerton. He went with the view of aiding us in our special work at Agra. In the same year he was made Principal of the school, Mr. Fullerton not wishing to retain the office, but continuing ready to relieve and assist him in any emergency. We had secured the services of an East Indian young gentleman, well qualified for the office of head master, and of other assistants; so that, though Mr. Williams' work must be onerous for a time, it is to be hoped that he may finally arrange to have but little of the actual teaching to do, and may be able to give his time to the Hindú controversy, for which his great learning and talents abundantly qualify him.

The school has grown till it has nearly one hundred

pupils; some of them from the Panjáb, on the one side, and some from Benares, on the other—a fact that shows the importance of the school to the country. It pays all its current expenses. Amongst the pupils are some native boys of good family, whose parents, though not Christians, wish their boys to be brought up with those who speak English, and have English manners and morals. For this purpose they pay more than the rates of the Government College, and take the risk of their sons being converted. Were it not that English and East Indian parents would object to a very great intermixture of heathen boys with theirs, we might, no doubt, have many more native boys. They learn the Catechism, read the Bible, stand at prayers, and receive the same religious instruction as the Christian boys.

It may be asked by our friends, as it was by the immersionists at Agra, why we should set up a Protestant school there, when there was already one belonging to the Baptist minister. The reasons—its comparative inefficiency, its expensiveness, and the want of security for its permanence—have already been mentioned. In regard to the latter, it ought to be added, that any place like the principalship of such a school cannot be so easily filled in India as in America, on the occurrence of a vacancy. Outside of the missions, proper men can rarely be found. This will not always be so: our school, and similar ones in Calcutta, will raise up a class of men and women fit for instructing their fellow-countrymen; but until this work be accomplished, help must be given to them by the missions. These views, however, were not acceptable to parties, whose private and sectarian interests were injured by our action. I was loudly accused of setting up the school out of mere sectarian spite. It was in vain for me to plead, that neither the scheme, nor the order for its execution, was evoked by me. The most absurd and uncharitable motives were ascribed to

me; and I was treated as the enemy of a party, and
the sole cause of all the injury they feared. They
could not see the least force in the public grounds
assigned for our action. But in the midst of their
opposition to our scheme, its policy was sadly vindi-
cated by the sudden death of the owner of their school.
Various strenuous efforts were made to keep up his
school, after his death; but they all failed, and in the
course of a few months it was totally abolished. We
of course regretted the death of the Baptist minister.
He had been a useful and good man, with whom it was
painful to come into collision; although we did not
think him and his friends right in the opposition they
offered.

A female school was considered scarcely less necessary than that for boys. Mr. Scott's scheme contem-
plated both; but our instructions from home were only
as to one. But Divine Providence immediately began
to press us onward in further measures for the education of that class of people. Two intelligent European
girls were taken in hand by Mrs. Fullerton, and partly
supported by some good ladies, in order to save them
from being sent to the Nunnery school. A poor East
Indian widow begged of Mrs. Fullerton to allow her
two daughters to attend also. Then some neighbours,
who could pay for the privilege, begged to be allowed
to send in their children. This Mrs. Fullerton was
induced to concede, so that she might hire some assistant. She procured the attendance of a young woman,
and began a private school, not promising to continue
it longer than it should suit her own convenience. She
soon had fifteen pupils.

This little beginning excited attention. There was
a good lady at Agra, the wife of a civilian, whose
name I would insert here did I not believe my doing
so would be disagreeable to her, who looked about to
see what other girls there might be who were unable
to pay for an education. She soon found several.

18*

Moved by what she had discovered, she begged donations and monthly subscriptions, got two other ladies
to join her to form a committee for the working of
her scheme, and took all the poor girls upon her fund,
including those whom Mrs. Fullerton had already admitted, in order to leave her more means for procuring
efficient assistance. This lady was so successful that in
a short time she had a fund of about twelve hundred
rupees, and monthly subscriptions nearly enough to
cover the monthly outlay. This fund, and similar
efforts in favour of poor boys, have since been amal-
gamated, as already intimated.

During the summer in which this informal school
grew up, two things occurred that bore upon our
schemes. The appointment of Mr. Williams was announced, accompanied with the intimation that he
would occupy the apartments in the boys' school-
house; and money was sent from New York for the
purchase of a house for Mr. Fullerton's family. At
the same time the prospect was held out to us of having more force attached to our station; and a direction
was indicated, in which it was hoped that the mission
might extend the sphere of its operations. This
movement seemed to promise that our forces would
be so kept up, that the addition of a girls' school to
our engagements would not embarrass us. But at the
same time the Executive Committee had informed us
that they could not sanction the establishment of this
school. And yet, since this seemed to be said rather
with a view to any expense that might be entailed
upon the committee by such an undertaking, we did
not consider it to be quite prohibited, if it could be
supported without incurring additional expenditure.

At the same time the prosperity of the school, the
predictions of friends, and the urgency of all concur-
ring circumstances, were such that we felt a good
degree of assurance that the Executive Committee
would soon be induced to order the full establishment

of the school. And if this should be done, and we, in the mean time, were to invest the money sent for an additional mission-house in a building only large enough for a family, we should at once be embarrassed by the want of a place in which to keep the school. The circumstances again made us feel that it was proper to proceed without instructions. I was again reluctant to assume such responsibility as was involved in setting on foot a permanent school without authority from home; but again my wife formed a scheme, and prepared to exert herself for my aid, and pressed me forward in what seemed to be the path of duty. We learned that a house, situated on the opposite side of the road from the boys' school, and well suited to our purpose, was for sale. We ascertained the lowest terms, and the latest day of payment. Then we determined to ask the advice and assistance of English friends, and to be guided by the developments of Providence. I went again to see Mr. Thomason, and stated all the circumstances to him. He said that he thought we ought to go on;—that I was, indeed, a *servant* of the Executive Committee, and bound to obey orders; but that I was also an *agent*, and could, in this case, do them better service by acting without orders;—and that our scheme had his most decided approval, and he would give us five hundred rupees towards buying the house. We then secured larger donations than before from the English residents at that and some other stations; and a particular effort amongst the class of people, for whose daughters the school was mainly intended, was quite successful. The Presbyterian church at Agra also gave me five hundred rupees towards this scheme, as a further acknowledgment of my services for the first year. For a time we were quite anxious as to the result; but I was led to persevere. The scheme, involving the expenditure of more than twice the money furnished from home for the house, was completed. I acquired the name of the *biggest beggar in North India;* but was sure that it was not applied to me in contempt, but rather indicated an increased degree of confidence and affection. This scheme afterward received the countenance of our Executive Committee; and the school flourishes so as to give good hope of its continuance.

The premises of the two schools are sufficiently near together to make them quite convenient for the mission, and yet so separated that the boys are quite separate from the girls. Together they present an imposing appearance. The cost of them was a considerable sum; but the community that aided us to buy them, and gave us about two-thirds of their cost, knew what we were doing, and would hardly have advised and assisted us to do it, unless they had thought the outlay a judicious one.

The girls' school is partly for day scholars, but boarders are kept in it. At first we did not intend that the boys' school should be so; but it was soon found that it would be desirable to have the head master keep a boarding-house. Accordingly we encouraged him to buy a house, the yard of which joined that of the boys' school. This will make his situation somewhat better than the salary which we could give him; and it secures a place for boys from a distance under our own control, while we escape the main trouble and anxiety attending it.

It is but right to mention the zeal and devotedness of Mrs. Fullerton in connection with the girls' school. The labour involved in the care and instruction of the school is very great, and the responsibility of the care of female boarders would not be easily borne, without any pecuniary recompense, by any one less heartily engaged in the Master's service. She has displayed the greatest patience under misconstructions and evil reports, even bearing to be asked if she considered her work to be missionary work. But she has already an instalment of her reward: spiritual fruit has been produced; and the marvellous transformation of character which results from her influence over the girls must be highly gratifying.

Our operations at Agra have produced some incidental effects. A number of gentlemen joined us, during the cold season of 1853-4, in giving a miscellaneous course of lectures to the English-speaking community. This effort was suggested by our mission, but it was taken up with so much spirit by all classes that the credit of it may fairly be considered public property. The gentlemen concerned did me the honour to invite me to give the opening lecture. The lectures were delivered in our boys' schoolhouse. Our good friend, the Hon. J. Thomason, Esq., Lieutenant-Governor of the Northwest Provinces, having died a very short time before, I took this occasion, with the consent of the mission, to introduce a short eulogium of him, mentioning him in connection with our schools, and dedicating the house, in which we were assembled, to his memory, by naming it " *Thomason Hall.*" Almost immediately after this, my connection with Agra was closed by my departure to visit America.

This account of the Agra schools has been given to show the liberality of the Indian Christian community, our relations with that community, and the nature of a part of our work at that particular station. The effect of labours, which we may expect to see, if they are followed up with perseverance, may be estimated by the account of the East Indians and the uncovenanted service, which is contained in this work. The influence of the strictly European portion of the community will always be very fluctuating; a station may at one time have three or four good men, or some excellent ladies, who will form society on their own model to a great extent; and in a short time they may all be gone to other stations, and persons of a quite different character may fill their places. The East Indian people are not strangers, serving a certain number of years in the country, but are settled in it; and therefore a given amount of help and influence derived from them annually is worth more to us than the same from those who are much higher in the scale of society, because it is more permanent. It is this fact that makes the thorough evangelization of this class of people so important.

Those who have had patience to follow me to this point, will thank God for the good that accrues to our missions from the English and other Christians in India; and they who know how sure all good is to be accompanied by evil in this world, will not be surprised to hear that some hinderances to our work arise from the same sources. According to my design, fully to display our circumstances in India, I will briefly mention the chief hinderances that are caused by those who are known to the heathen as Christians.

There are usually within the field of our missions about six thousand European troops, besides the regiments of natives officered by Europeans. There are a few of these soldiers who are good men; but the immense majority of the privates are ignorant and depraved, perhaps to a greater extent than any other class of Englishmen in the world. They are recruited from the worst classes, and in India they are almost entirely freed from the moral restraints that surround them, and must influence them more or less, at home. Drunkenness and licentiousness strongly mark their conduct, whenever they can escape from the immediate restraints of military discipline. It is impossible to keep the natives from knowing their characteristics. Again and again are their character and conduct flung at the missionary; and we are advised to go to them, and not have the impertinence to recommend our religion to others, until it has reformed our own people. We are obliged, in this and some similar cases, to explain that there are two kinds of Christians—those who are simply called so from the nation or tribe they were born in, and those who are so by real faith. The only effectual way that I could ever find to answer the objection, was to say that our religion makes those who are under its power really better men; while the Mohammedan and Hindú faiths only make men self-righteous, and conceitedly devout, and malignantly bigoted. We can appeal to so many examples of all kinds, that our answer is not without its power, though it certainly does not fully neutralize the influence of wicked Europeans. Though there are a few good men in almost every regiment, and they are known to the officers, yet they are scarcely known to the natives, and have no influence on them. They hardly ever learn the language of the country, and their example is quite unknown and unnoticed.

A large proportion of the East Indians formerly had the vices of both their parent races, and the virtues of neither. The drunkenness of the European, the duplicity of the Hindustání, and the weakness of a newly mixed race, formed a very undesirable character. Professing Christianity, and practising many native customs, they did the native religions no harm, while they compromised ours before the native community. These people are now greatly improved, and there are most estimable persons amongst them. They marry mostly amongst themselves, and concubinage with native women is almost at an end. Their ranks have recently also been recruited from a better stock than formerly. But many representatives of their former character are still found. Many of the musicians of native infantry regiments, and some of the lowest of the copyists about the public offices, are still specimens of the class referred to; and here and there, scattered through the country, some are to be found *sharking* for a living. Their reputation is not favourable to Christianity. They are often referred to by our opponents; but we are able to refer to many who are an honour to our religion. This class is increasing, and further labour on their behalf will still more increase their good influence.

Too many military officers do us harm by their example. It is true, that the officers are generally a most respectable body of men; but there are exceptions, and all exceptions are keenly noted by the natives. The notorious licentiousness of some, and the unscrupulous indebtedness of others, are unfavourable to our labours, for the same reason that the vices of European soldiers are so; and some of them actively oppose us. I have known the case of an officer, detached for civil employment, who had an intelligent Musalmán in his office, on whom a strong impression had been made by our labours at Allahabad. This man asked the officer's advice about making a profession of Christianity, expecting encouragement to do so. He judged that a Christian would naturally like to see one converted to his religion; but he was surprised to meet with abuse. The officer called him a fool; asked him why he should change his religion, when one was as good as another; and told him that he had no right to do it, because he was born a Mohammedan, which was, therefore, what God had intended him to be. When the man argued that but one of the two faiths could be true, the officer called him a hog, and told him to mind his work. But such gross examples as this are rare. More harm is done by the prevailing levity and wildness of young officers, and by the general negative example of irreligion set by the great body of the army. But here we most thankfully note exceptions: there are those who honour Christianity, and labour for its advancement. And the domestic relations of officers are now much more creditable to Christianity than they formerly were.

Though it is perfectly a digression, I will not scruple to say something more of the Mohammedan

mentioned in the preceding paragraph. The close of
his history is covered with impenetrable obscurity.
He was near being baptized by us, when he took a
temporary leave of absence from the office in which
he served, and went to see his family; and he
never returned. He could not have stayed away to
escape baptism; for he was not so committed to us
that he could not have drawn back if he pleased.
He would not run away from his service, for he
could get nothing equal to it in worldly advantage
anywhere else. We heard a report from the neighbourhood of his family, that after he had been with
his friends a few days, his brothers gathered his
cousins together, and two or three more staunch
Mohammedans, and disputed with him till late at
night. When the discussion had heated their temper,
his elder brother solemnly called on him to abjure
Christ, and promise not to be baptized. He answered,
" I will die first." " Die, then!" shouted his furious
brother, and cut him down with a sword. This story
could not be authenticated; but his disappearance is
otherwise unaccounted for. When the present dis-
pensation is closed up, perhaps we shall see him and
many more such martyrs amongst "the host of
God's elect." And we shall be rewarded for our
labour if our mission shall be the means of sending
but one such there.

Merchants, speculators, and travellers in India
have exerted an evil influence. Planters also are
often a stumbling-block. There have been examples
of knavery, oppression, and vice, rivalling the utmost
depths of native depravity. Native bankers cannot
pretend to equal some of the transactions of English
banks in that country. But here, again, there are
redeeming points; there are men of these classes who
have been an honour and a blessing to the country.

Civilians have generally set a better example than
other classes of the European community. More of

19

them are married men, and live regularly and virtu-
ously. They are not all such as they ought to be;
and occasionally one of them does more harm to
Christianity than several good men can repair.

Members of all classes of the nominally Christian
community do us a mischief by compliances with the
native religions. On one occasion an officer of high
rank visited a Hindú shrine near us, and when
solicited by the priests, gave them sixteen rupees.
He probably only desired a reputation for liberality;
but, instead of that, he got the reputation amongst
the natives of having a sneaking regard for, and
some fear of, the idol worshipped there. He knew
that his donation would be considered an offering to
the idol; but he laughed at objections, saying, " Let
the poor devils think what they will."

Sometimes we have trials that arise from good
men. Difficulties with assistants have been increased
by their injudicious interference. A wicked (or
crazy) apostate baptized Bráhman has been paid for
preaching for years, by a good old General, who
would not believe that his protegé preached against
Christianity. There have been cases of interference
in mission affairs by friends, which produced difficulty
and embarrassment. I have known good men, who
evidently expected us to consider their immense
salaries and high official positions to be good arguments in any discussion. But it would be ungracious
to dwell on the faults of the friends of our cause,
even if we do suffer from them sometimes.

The writing of this chapter has given me pleasure.
There are sad things in it, as there are in all parts
of this world's history. But in this case the good
predominates. The influence of the English in India
is in favour of, rather than against Christianity.
And amongst the East Indians, and others who will
make India their home, there will arise labourers to
convert the natives, and supporters and comforters of

those labourers, concerning whom it shall be clearly
written, " the wilderness and the solitary place shall
be glad for them."

CHAPTER IX.

SUCCESS.

IT is but natural that all, who care anything about
missions, should ask, What is the effect of all these
operations, that are detailed and alluded to in this
volume?—and it is but reasonable that I should give
them as clear an idea of it as I have tried to give of
our situation and labours. Something will already
have been gathered from the preceding chapters; for
the personal anecdotes that I have related, contain
accounts of some of our converts, and allude to
more. I most heartily wish that I could tell a more
stirring story of our successes than the truth will
allow me to do. It would gladden the hearts of the
missionaries to be able to report crowds of inquirers
coming, and great numbers baptized; it would save
them from many an hour of heaviness, if they could
see more souls given to them for their hire; and it
would doubtless stir up the activity of the Church at
home to hear such accounts. But though we cannot
tell of many having "believed our report," yet there
is no reason for discouragement. There are two considerations that ought to have great weight in estimat-
ing the value of our success.

There has not yet elapsed sufficient time to secure
any great amount of success. Every one, who has
read accounts of missions, knows that from fifteen to
twenty-five years pass in preliminary labour before

there is much fruit gathered. Those places that
have been most distinguished by the blessings poured
out upon them, have been cultivated with this amount
of assiduous patience. If any one studies the missions in Southern India, from the time of Schwartz
onward, he will find that at first the amount of success was only sufficient to keep the labourers in heart
and hope; and the field, where now the Episcopal
and the Independent English, and the American
Board missionaries are receiving village after village
under their care for instruction in Christianity, formerly supplied only families and individuals singly,
with crosses, difficulties, and frequent defections.
The history of the missions in the Sandwich and
Society Islands is so well known, that they only need
to be alluded to as cases in point. The missions in
the Turkish Empire, though now their successes are
sufficient to be thought one cause of the Russian
movement in that direction, went through a long
night of faith before they were favoured with such
results. The Church missions in Bengal had been
longer planted than any of ours, before the Krishnagar movement gave indications of approaching day;
and then they received, as we may say, at once, four
thousand converts. And beside the actual converts,
the influence of the truth has produced a sect amongst
the natives, called *Kartá-Bhojás*, (worshippers of the
Creator,) said to number one hundred thousand souls.
These men have cast off idolatry, and are much more
accessible than others. They, in fact, occupy the
position of a compromise between the truth and
idolatry, to which they are brought by the combined
action of the truth on the one side, and the pride of
the natural heart on the other; they *cannot* remain
in gross heathenism; they *will not*, if they can avoid
it, submit to the humbling doctrines of Christianity.
We hope that their present stand is but temporary.
And how long is it since the first Protestant mission-

aries went to China? Well might the faint-hearted have asked, When shall we see a result? But the Chinese rebellion has shown that the truth has produced an effect—not altogether that which we would have desired—but one that at least shows that idolatry has been shaken to its foundations, and leaves, or will leave, the field clear for building up the truth on the *debris* of error.

The second consideration is, that we have a greater amount of difficulties to contend with in India than perhaps anywhere else. Take into view first those mentioned in the preceding chapter, and those that are common to all our race of aliens from God. Then let us try to realize the obstruction thrown in our way by *caste*. All have heard of the four great castes of Hindús; and some may have thought that there must be many people who are not comprehended in any of these, and therefore will be without the trammels of this institution. And this was, no doubt, at first intended to be the operation of the system; or perhaps it was intended by its founders, that all who fell from the higher castes should find a place in the lowest. But men can never fully calculate beforehand what will be the effect of their policy; and probably the priestly caste little dreamed, when they settled their system of ranks, that outcasts and foreigners would so far follow their example as to band themselves in castes in imitation of them. But this has happened—quarrels have split castes, the one party excommunicating the other; but neither party has forsaken the institution of caste—they have simply formed two instead of one. And these have again divided and subdivided, till no man knows their number. Mistakes or omissions in their ritual have put Bráhmans out of communion with the great body; but they have been able to form parties, and to retain the exercise of the priestly office in some places, though not allowed to be Bráhmans in others; and

19*

thus an endless variety of Bráhmans is to be found. Illegitimacy has been the fruitful parent of new castes. Even the *dead* have formed a caste:—there is a town in Bengal, where those live who have recovered after being carried to the river to die. They are judicially dead according to Hindú law; and here they have settled, intermarried, have children, and observe caste amongst themselves, as much as if they had never lost caste, or had originated from one caste. There are a multitude of those whose parents lost caste ages ago, and they have banded together and formed new ones. The Mohammedans have fallen into the same custom, and are as careful to preserve a certain distance from others, totally uncommanded by the Koran, as any Hindús. Caste is genteel in Upper India. It is an appendage to character which no man is willing to own that he lacks. The effect of all this is, that no one is so low as to have nothing to lose by joining us. The question continually occurs, What shall we do out of caste? And indeed it is a fearful thing to lose the privilege of ever eating again with parents, brothers and sisters, and other relatives, or of entering the house, or of aiding in sickness, or assisting to bury— to be cut off from all sympathy, and to become an object of detestation and loathing in exact proportion to the affection formerly enjoyed; and that too before the party the person joins is large enough to give security for some equivalent to these ruptured ties. Thus until the native Christians become so numerous as to form a recognized community by themselves, here will be a very great hinderance to the constitutionally timid, and to the weak in faith. Of all other mission fields ours most resembles the Turkish empire in this respect. The old churches there are like the castes in India in many things, especially in the unsocial way in which dissidents are treated.

And still another great obstruction is found in the

religious and philosophical systems of the country, and in its pseudo-civilization. It is not in the same situation as the barbarous islands were, which had lost all confidence in their idols, and presented, as nearly as possible, a *tabula rasa*, on which to write a new faith. In India there is a high and romantic mythology, to give character to its idolatry, presenting the grossest idolatry to the lowest, a gross polytheism to the half-educated, and a refined and philosophical pantheism to the higher classes. The doctrines of both the Mohammedans and the Hindús are well suited to the corrupt propensities of human nature—both to those of the low and gross, and to those of the lovers of self-righteousness and spiritual pride. The priesthood, instead of being mere ignorant mummers, are intelligent men, with so much knowledge as easily to impose on the masses and exercise a great influence. India has a history, both political and literary; and our attempt is to overthrow both opinions and a social system, which are the growth of ages, and are connected with a certain and well defined form of civilization. The attempt is sublime in its magnitude. No political revolution that was ever attempted half equals it. Were not our dependence on something infinitely higher than the power of man, this attempt would not have hope enough to make it ridiculous—it would be simply beneath contempt. We are certainly superior to the people of India in learning and civilization; but not so superior as to have the advantage given by the immeasurable distance between Europeans and savages. We have something more to do than to clear the ground and build: we have first to pull down.

I have already mentioned the baptism of the first native convert at Allahabad as having occurred the first summer after my arrival. Within the next year one of the catechists whom I have mentioned was received. From that time to the present, now and then one has been received from the Hindús and the Mohammedans, and several from the orphan asylums. The ratio of conversions is increasing. Scarcely a month passes now, in which the accession of some one or more to our churches is not reported. Some native Christians have been received from other places; some have been dismissed to other churches; and several have died. There are now about forty native communicants, including some assistants who have been sent to out-stations; and about double this number have been members of the church in all. The whole native community gathered there is about one hundred and fifty, including the children in the orphan asylums. The history of all other missionary stations in North India, so far as my acquaintance extends, is similar to this in regard to accessions. Some have had more, some less. At some of them greater facilities exist for giving employment to converts than at others. While at Agra I sent the inquirers from that place to Futtehgurh for this reason. The members of our churches are not, of course, all equally satisfactory as to character. Some of them are without much zeal and activity as Christians; and some are weak and stumbling Christians, too selfish, too worldly, too unsteady. So were some of the converts of the Apostles; and when this cannot be said of a great many Christians in America, then I will enter upon such an apology as may be made for these in Hindustán. And some of our people really are very good people, and profit by the means of grace. They are not all that we should desire, but they are a light amongst the heathen. To show what some of them are, I will refer the reader to an article of mine, written for one of the missionary periodicals, and republished by the Board of Publication, entitled "Poor Blind Sally." It gives an account of a blind girl, who, through love of the Scriptures, made astonishing progress in learning English from a single gospel, the only book we could then procure for her in the raised characters. Her spiritual attainments are set forth in that little work in such a light, that any reader of it will see that our labour is not fruitless. Another case is that of the young man, who went from our church to Agra with Mr. Wilson. Mr. Wilson published a notice of him when he died, which testifies to his sweet Christian character. Many a mourner for a dear brother has sorrowed less than did Mr. Wilson over the loss of this humble brother, whose body was the first planted in the yard of the new Presbyterian church at Agra. As another specimen of the work of grace amongst our people, I copy the following from a notice of Jatní, a deceased member of our church. It was written for childen, and for that reason may have too little dignity of style for some readers; but I prefer not to alter it much.

"You have, no doubt, often heard of happy deaths amongst Christians at home. Some of you have lost a father, or mother, or other dear friends, who have called you to their bedside, and have given you good advice, and taken leave of you. You may remember how your dear departed mother, in the paleness and weakness of approaching death, still looked happy; and how her friends crowded around her bed with tears of sorrow and smiles of joy on their countenances—sorrow, that one so dear was about to be taken away; and joy, because she by faith could 'see heaven opened, and the Son of Man standing on the right hand of God.' You would not, perhaps, understand all that you saw; and your little hearts would be bursting with grief and fear. But still you can understand enough to know, that true religion will give great comfort in the hour of death. This is so frequently seen in your favoured country, that if the death, which has occurred here, had taken place there, I should not have thought of writing about it for you. But, as I said before, it is in some points a new thing

here.   And I will tell you about it, so that you may
see that true piety is the same thing everywhere.   I
wish also that you should see, that God blesses your
missionaries, at least in some degree.   We do not yet
see the desert blossom as the rose-garden, from the
refreshing showers of the Spirit of grace; but we are
permitted to see, now and then, a rose springing up,
and opening out its beauties, to show us that the seed
is taking root in the ground; and that it is the *right*
seed, of our Father's planting, and not merely the
seed of tares, sown by an enemy.

"Many years ago, a Bráhman, named Ranjít, made
a profession of Christianity at Chunar, and put himself under the care of the late Rev. W. Bowley.   There
he was baptized, and after a while made a catechist,
or native assistant.   He was engaged some years as
superintendent of a village belonging to the Church
mission at Chunar.   We hope he was a true Christian;
but it is painful to have to say, that he was not at all
times so consistent as it is necessary and desirable a
Christian man should be.   We must remember that he
had been brought up a heathen till he became a man;
and more, that he was a Bráhman—a caste that has
some temptations and some vices that are peculiar to
them, but which are the necessary result of their being
worshipped as gods by the common people.   He died
several years ago.

" This man had two daughters, of the younger of
whom I am about to tell you.   She was married, when
about fifteen years old, to one of the young men who
had been brought up at that mission; and they were
shortly after sent to us by Mr. Bowley, for employment.   Her husband has since become the foreman of
the printing-office under my care here.   Both these
persons were educated in connection with Mr. Bowley's
orphan schools.   They were not orphans, but taught
with the orphans.

" You must understand, that we do not allow any

distinctions of caste amongst the Christians; they all visit each other, and eat together on such occasions, without making any difficulty about it. The Hindús call them *Bhrasht*, for this; that is, depraved, spoiled. But we teach them that only sin makes any one *bhrasht;* we tell them that nothing but good and bad conduct, and more or less education, ought to make any distinctions amongst men. Our people generally get on very well together; but you will not be surprised to hear that Satan sometimes tempts one and another of them to fancy themselves more genteel by birth than others. I remember very well, when I was a boy at school, as many of you are now, how some of us used to feel, because we lived in better houses, or had better clothes, or our fathers were rather more respectable than those of some others; and sometimes, when we were naughty enough to quarrel, we reproached others. I am ashamed of it now, whenever I think of it. I dare say some of you have done the same thing; and I hope you will soon be ashamed of it too. In this way I have known one to say here, 'I am the son of a Bráhman, and your father was only a weaver; do you think to make yourself equal with me?' And another would say, 'I am a Rájpút by birth, and your father was a cobbler; so what impertinence it is in you to think of disputing with me.' But this has very seldom happened, and for some years past scarcely at all. Our people are from almost every caste, and they get on together as peaceably as any community I ever knew.

"The young woman of whom I am writing, was the daughter of a man of the very highest caste. Had her father continued in Hindúism, his daughter, while playing with the little girls of the village, might have taken their playthings away, or called them bad names, or pushed them, and they would not have dared to say anything. No children in your country can treat others so tyrannically as the high caste children here can the low caste. She might have been worshipped; there are various times when the virgin daughters of Bráhmans are worshipped especially. And it is altogether probable that sometimes she had thoughts of pride come into her mind about the fact that her father was a Bráhman.

"This young woman was baptized in her childhood by the name of Betsey; but was also frequently, indeed generally, called by her native name, Jatní. She was received to the communion in our church, five or six years ago. At that time she passed an examination; but we did not see anything very remarkable in her. She was so modest, so shame-faced, that she never could, while in health, talk with us very freely. I have often noticed, that she seemed to pay perfect attention to the preaching of the gospel; and when I have been in her house to speak on the subject of religion, she always seemed to listen with great interest, and to be glad of the opportunity to learn. If I asked her any questions, she answered me in a satisfactory manner, so far as her extreme modesty, or timidity, would permit her to speak. But though so shy, it was not long before we discovered that her character had many excellencies. Though we could not often hear of anything in particular that she did, yet she gained the respect and love of all the native Christian community. All the men were ready to point to her as an example for their wives; and all the women, without envy or strife, acknowledged her as the most excellent person amongst them. The customs of this country almost entirely forbid a respectable woman speaking to a man out of her own family; and Jatní was too unfeignedly modest to find fault with the custom, or transgress against it. So her influence was not brought to bear upon the men as that of a good woman so often is in America. But this was more the fault of circumstances than of herself. On one occasion, one of our young men had been guilty of some bad conduct, and

I had thought it necessary to punish him. At first he resented it, and said he would not remain here; but he went on some errand to Jatní's house, and she asked him about his circumstances. He told her his griefs; and she told him how sin had brought them all upon him. She besought him not to go away. Her kindness brought him to tears and confession. He went to his work again, and has been a better man ever since. But her life was short; and the history of a quiet, modest, retiring female is soon written; it would not be so easy a task to write out an account of all the lovely traits of her character.

"Now all this is in such marked and beautiful contrast to the life of an ordinary native woman, that I love to dwell upon it. The heathen women are without education, and without useful employment, aside from cooking for their families. Their time is spent in useless chatter, or clamorous quarrelling. A man would consider it the last and deepest disgrace to be known to have asked a woman's advice, or to have followed it when offered. Such a thing as a woman gaining influence for good, in a Hindú community, has not been known for the last two thousand years. But here was a woman, from amongst that very people, who, without effort, was a shining light to the full extent of her sphere; and without seeking it, exercised an influence on all around her. I gratefully acknowledge that, humble as she was, I valued the friendship she bore to my family. The last tears I saw on her face were shed when she sent her blessing to my little boy in America. Very pleasant was she to us. She never quarrelled, nor slandered, nor excited differences, but was a healer of divisions. The difference between her and her heathen countrywomen must have been seen, in order to be known; and all this was in such beautiful quietness and modesty, such feminine, and even lady-like delicacy. This woman was of the *second generation* of Christians. The faults that I have

20

hinted at, as existing in her father, did not appear in her. The benefit of early education in Christianity is here most manifest. Nearly all our hopes are placed on the generations to come, whose mothers shall have been Christians.

"Jatní suffered many sorrows in her life. She had a darling little son. He was 'black, but comely.' It may be that you will be scarcely able to believe me when I say, that I have not seen five handsomer babies in my life than was little Abraham, black though he was; but it is quite true. He was finely formed, with a skin of the most perfectly healthy hue; his hair so fine, and his large, speaking, black eyes so pleasant. His head was most beautiful in shape. You may well believe that he was his mother's joy. At thirteen months of age he was suddenly cut down by convulsions, after about a day's illness. My wife and I saw him die. Poor Jatní, who was not at all prepared for such an event, cast her arms around Mrs. Warren's waist, and hid her face in her bosom, and in a strain very similar to David's lament for Absalom, bemoaned her loss. But she neither did nor said anything unbecoming her Christian profession. After this she had another little boy, almost as fine a child as little Abraham, who died in the same way; and after this again a little daughter. On one of these occasions, for a few moments, she was almost wild with grief; but when I began to hold up to her view the heaven that is promised to believers and their infant children, she at once laid hold of and acknowledged the consolations of the gospel.

"At last came sickness—fever, constantly returning in spite of all that could be done to check it. I suspected *consumption*, and soon it showed itself in a way that left no doubt but that we should soon lose her. I took the first favourable opportunity to ask her how she felt when the question came up in her mind, whether she should get well or not. I asked this with all the care and softness that I could; because I knew she was so timid, and I feared she might be shocked and injured. But I was delighted to find that she had thought of it, and had come to feel willing that God should do with her, as to life, just as he pleased. I questioned her closely, and set death and the judgment before her plainly; but her nerves were firm, her eye clear, and her voice calm and steady: her uniform profession, from that time forward, was, 'I know Christ, and can fully and completely trust him in all things. He keeps my mind in perfect peace.' No soldier on the field of battle, and no brave and strong man in danger, ever faced death with more cool, unwavering courage, than did this weak, timid, shrinking woman, though shattered by sickness and pain. I saw her often, and always found her the same.

"Her disease was not very rapid in its destructive work. She wasted away for some months; sometimes she had hope of recovery; but that hope did not produce any lessening of her resignation, nor did it seem to render her less fit for her great change. At length she gave up all hope. I saw very little difference in her after this. She seemed to be ready to go; and the main thing that I could notice in the state of her mind, was a quiet, calm, trustful waiting for the set time. At last, one Saturday evening, I saw that she was very near her end. I talked with her about the work that the Saviour still had for her to do; and told her to pray for grace to speak and testify for him to the last. I gave orders to be called during the night, if she should seem to be dying. But she lived throughout Sunday. I went to see her before going to church on Sunday evening, and found that she was peaceful. When I returned from church she was dead.

"As soon as it was known that I had come into

my bungalow, my best native Christian assistant
came to tell me of it. To my surprise, he spoke in
a tone of unusual animation, and he seemed rejoicing.
I asked, 'How did she die?' 'O, sir, such a thing
was never seen in the native Christian community in
this part of the country before. She called for you,
and was sorry she could not tell you how much she
thanked you for all you had taught her, and com-
forted her. Then she called for all of us, and when
we went to her, she asked, if she had offended any
one; and said, that if she had, she begged for pardon. Then she said, she wanted to tell us that
Christ was with her, and that her heart was full of
joy and faith. Then she bade us all farewell, and
prayed for us. We all knelt down and prayed for
her. She spoke to her heathen servant, and told
him to become a Christian. Then she remained
silent a few moments, and suddenly died.' I said,
'This is a very happy thing that has occurred,
Baboo. This is not like a common death, that leaves
a faint hope and a great deal of sorrow behind.'
'No, sir; it is not. Come out and see the people.
You will see how those who loved her best rejoice
rather than mourn.' I went out, and found a large
party of the Christians gathered in the verandah.
The body was laid out there. All were calm. I
talked to them a little about what they had witnessed.
Many of them confessed, that when they had heard
from us how happily Christians had died, they had
hardly been able to believe it; but now they had seen
it—it was a strange thing to them. They had known
Christians to die with some calmness; but they had
never seen one triumphant and joyful.

"The next day we laid the body of dear Jatní
beside those of her three children. After the prayer
at the side of the grave, one of the native Christians,
apparently from a strong impulse, took up, in the
Hindustání language, the beautiful words of the

Episcopal burial service—beautiful when said over the grave of a true believer—'Forasmuch as it hath pleased Almighty God, of his great mercy, to take unto himself the soul of our dear sister, here departed, we therefore commit her body to the ground; earth to earth, ashes to ashes, dust to dust; in sure and certain hope of the resurrection to eternal life, through our Lord Jesus Christ.' Then we all sprinkled some clay on her coffin, and left her 'body, still united to Christ, to rest in the grave till the resurrection.'

"What a glorious faith is the Christian's! Dear reader, 'What think you of Christ?' Is he worth following? Will you ever be able to find another friend that can so stand by you in your greatest extremity.

"What think you of preaching Christ? It was preaching Christ that produced these scenes, of which I have been writing. What do you think would have been the end of Jatní without the gospel? Sullen stupidity and hardness of heart—the death of a beast; or raving fear, calling on idols for help, and finding none; or blaspheming anger against the gods, for so soon calling her away from life. These are common ways in which death is met in this country. And what would her friends have done without the gospel? They would have jumped about as if fire were being applied to their limbs, and would have screamed like mad people; and would have beaten their heads against the side of the bedstead or the walls of the house; their eyes would have rolled about, while they beat their breasts and tore their hair. I have seen all this. Who, then, would say we ought not to send the gospel to India?

"Give me to appear before the great white throne, with but one such Indian diamond in my crown, if it may be no more, and I am content!"

I have given this obituary thus at length, because I

20*

could not see what to leave out. I could much more
easily add more. These also are not all the cases
that could be brought forward. All our missions
have witnessed scenes of peace on the death-bed, if
not of triumph. But I desire not to weary my readers, and therefore will not do more in this particular
direction; though I am well aware that true Christians are more pleased with such exhibitions of spiritual fruit than with any other indications of success.

Though the salvation of individual souls is the
most pleasing proof of success, yet the general effect
of our labours on the country is by no means to be
left out of sight. Some persons may even think such
an effect of more consequence than any other form of
success; because, if Christianity be once planted
there, the salvation of souls will follow as a matter of
course. For this reason I will make as careful a
statement as possible of the influence on public ideas
which Christianity has gained.

Much has been gained by our religion by a general
impression having been created in its favour. Fifteen,
or even ten years ago a native Christian was esteemed a monster. A convert was not said to have
changed his religion, but to have *lost* it—to have become an infidel, or worse. Latterly this prejudice is
much abated, and the native Christians are acknowledged to have a religion. Once they were reviled,
pushed away from the wells and other public places,
and were a proverb for everything low. To become
a Christian, was, in the estimation of the public, to
throw off every restraint, to indulge every evil propensity, and to wallow in all degradation. The
Christian was known to regard no kind of food as
unholy, and therefore he was considered as worse
than even the Chamárs, who acknowledge some restraints, though they eat cattle that die of disease.
The only notion that was generally entertained as to
the restraints of religion, was that they related to

food and personal connections; but now the natives known that our religion inculcates a pure morality, self-denial, and labour for the good of others. Since this knowledge of Christianity has been spread abroad, as well as a general notion of its doctrines, the natives treat Christians with much more consideration, and look on our religion as something really respectable. It is a great thing to have been able to get the idea of a spiritual religion, and one that is connected with good morals, implanted in the general mind of the community. Along with this knowledge of our faith is widely spread the impression that it will ultimately prevail. We are often told by the natives that we shall finally uproot Hindúism; that the present generation will not be converted, but the next probably will, &c. These impressions afford us more facilities in preaching than we formerly enjoyed. Once Bráhmans could easily drive away an audience from us; now it is rarely attempted, and the attempt almost always fails. Once we were often opposed by certain other classes, who now usually avoid us. There were certain standing objections to Christianity and defences of Hindúism; which were often brought forward by our opponents, and are now generally abandoned. There were gross slanders current about our converts, such as that we bought their adhesion with money and women,* which are now obsolete, and seldom repeated. All these impressions, that have been made upon the mind of the country, are valuable. They are not *saving* impressions; and nothing short of these ought to satisfy us. Yet we are not to despise them. God is glorified when the religion of Christ is only recommended to men by its good fruits, Matt. v. 16. And this work has been done to such an extent that something like an excitement has been

---

* A favourite story used to be, that we had engaged to give each convert a *European wife*—such a wife being considered beyond measure valuable.

produced in different parts of the country. The work at Krishnagar has been referred to already, in which a multitude were converted. This is below our territory, and where missions have been maintained longer. In our region we have seen something approaching to it. Near Futtehgurh a village was for a time in a state that gave great hopes, and which caused very much talk in that region. This unhappily died away without the fruit that had been hoped for; but we still hope that some favourable effects of it will yet appear. Near Lodiana is a sect that professes to worship only Jesus. It derives its doctrines from our books, and adds to them. Probably there is much that is wrong and unchristian in this sect; but the movement is indicative of a ferment caused by the leaven of truth. We also hope that some of these people may yet be led to the truth by it. Other facts of this kind also show that our doctrines are spreading, and are producing effect—there is a shaking of the dry bones.

The effect that has been produced upon the prevailing ideas of caste ought to be noticed. Formerly when a person lost caste, he was not only socially avoided, but he was considered wicked and despicable. To speak to him was a disgrace. His relatives avoided him as they would the plague, and even hated him. He had not only lost his social position, but had brought a disgrace upon all his family. Caste was connected with religious, as well as with social, ideas. There has occurred a great change in this respect. Caste has not been abolished—perhaps is not near being so; but it has lost the character of holiness. If a man breaks its rules he is equally excluded now as formerly; but the exclusion now relates to the table, to intermarriage, and the like. It does not cause people to treat the outcast with scorn. They will not eat with him; but they content themselves with avoiding him in this and similar things.

He is rather treated as a stranger than a disgraced person. When I first went to India there were frequent cases that I was acquainted with, in which men fell under suspicion of having transgressed the rules of caste, and were always promptly suspended till they could prove their innocence or make atonement. The least suspicion alarmed the caste immediately, and they most jealously guarded their purity. An accused man had the burden of proof laid on him— no one was called to prove his offence, but he must prove his innocence. This whole thing is changed ˅ now. The Hindús have grown so indifferent to the old ideas of the holiness of caste, that they do not care how much a man may be suspected. Let him eat what, and with whom, he will, and his compeers will deny and disbelieve it as long as possible. They will refuse to take up and examine the most probable charges. The whole burden of proof is laid on the accuser. We had a young Bráhman candidate for baptism, who several times ate and drank with us and our people, and afterward repented of his intention, and went away from us. It was often told to the members of his caste that he had broken caste, but they would take no cognizance of the case, unless a member of the caste would come forward as accuser, and produce eye-witnesses; and as none of us would go to give testimony, there could be no conviction. He told me, when I asked him about it, "They know that I should join with the Christians immediately if they put me out; and though they know I am totally a transgressor, for whom no atonement can be made, yet they do not choose to believe it." A native Christian woman of ours, at first despised and rigidly exiled by her family, was at length invited to visit them, and was visited by them at my place. They seemed to have very pleasant intercourse, save that the heathen relatives avoided eating with her. This relaxation of caste is very significant and important.

The institution may linger a while; but we may look for more and more infractions of its rules continually. The ideas of gentility, as connected with high birth, will cause the higher castes to claim consideration on account of it for a long time to come; but when it comes to be a mere sign of social rank, it will be only a chained lion in our way.

The general effects above spoken of, are evident from the number of persons that become inquirers for a time, and who, if they do not become converts to Christianity, probably assist much to spread a knowledge of its doctrines and spirit. There is hardly any time when each station has not one or more persons under special instruction. These persons are of all castes, and from all parts of the country. Some of them prove converts, and are admitted; some grow weary, and leave us when they find our religion so spiritual, and see that they have not the character we require, and do not like that character, and find that we have no ceremonies with which the conscience may be amused in the absence of a knowledge of the blood of sprinkling; and some come from worldly motives, play the hypocrite while it serves their purpose, and then go away. Some also are prevented from making a profession of Christianity by peculiar causes or infirmities. I will here give some personal anecdotes, which will show what is meant, better than these mere general statements. It will not be necessary, in this connection, to give the history of a convert; for these may be sufficiently gathered from other places. I will only mention some of those who have not yet made a profession of Christianity.

About seven years since, I visited a village thirty-five miles above Allahabad, on the bank of the Ganges. The village possesses peculiar interest from two facts. It formerly had a fort, which commanded the Ganges at that point, built upon an eminence of about one hundred and fifty feet—one of the only two considerable heights that I know of on the Upper Ganges. This fort was the stronghold of a Hindú king, and was taken, after a long siege, by one of the early Mohammedan emperors. An immense number of persons perished in the besieging army. The tradition is, that the number was only five less than a hundred thousand; and the Mohammedans say, that, as they all perished either in fighting for the faith, or in attendance on the army of the faithful, had there been only five more, to make up the round hundred thousand, the place would have become as holy as Mecca the Honourable. The burying-ground outside of the town is one of the most impressive of all scenes, presenting as complete a notion of the horrors of war as can be found. On battle-fields the dead are thrown into a common trench, and their graves do not afterwards suggest the details of the slaughter; but here, as the sword or the pestilence cut down one after another, they were separately buried, and a brick grave constructed for each, of different sizes and styles, corresponding to the different ranks. These graves remain, in all states of preservation and decay, covering a desolate plain of great extent, and forming a monument of the siege unequalled in size and appropriateness.

The other interesting fact is, that ever since the capture of that fortress, the town has been the residence of some Mohammedan families of distinction, which, though now much decayed, are still considered to belong to the principal aristocracy of the country. I visited some of these families, and preached there, beside holding disputations in two of their houses. I found that Mr. Scott, my associate in the voyage to India, had stopped there on his way to Futtehgurh, and had given them some tracts. A young man seemed much interested when I preached, and followed me around, offering me such polite attention as he could. Afterwards he visited me at my house repeatedly, held arguments, made inquiries, and read such books as I recommended. He made acquaintance with my native Christians, and received much instruction from the catechists. We had great hopes of him, and his friends considered him to have gone so far as to be unworthy of the social privileges of caste. They refused to eat or drink with him, till he should renounce intercourse with us. He continued in this way for several months, and professed to have entirely lost his belief in Mohammedanism; of the truth of which profession I have no doubt. He found difficulties in some of the doctrines of the New Testament, especially in that of the divinity of Christ. We could not persuade him to let the discussion of such points alone, till he had examined the main question, as to the authority of the gospel; but he would perplex himself with them. After exciting our hopes to the utmost, he gradually grew cool, and drew back; though he still professes friendship for us, and a general belief in Christianity. His friends were very anxious about him all the time that he was himself anxious; and they often visited us, and sought to put us down by argument. The excitement about this young man was the occasion of a great deal of preaching; and many of the friends of his family became acquainted with Christianity to a great extent. We still hope for good effects from this case.

On one Sabbath morning, I went to preach for one of the other missionaries at the mission church, leaving my assistant, Bábú Harí, to preach at the chapel connected with the printing-house. As I have before stated, this chapel faces the bázár road, and is often attended by Hindús and Mohammedans from curiosity. After I returned, Bábú Harí brought to me a young man, apparently about twenty-two years old, who had attended his preaching that morning, and afterwards called on him at his house. I noticed that the Bábú appeared much pleased; and on asking what had happened—what the young man wanted—I learned

that he had been found, after the service, looking at
the Bábú's house from a little distance, and expressing
a great desire to make his acquaintance. On being
introduced, he told the Bábú that he had long been
seeking the way of salvation; that ever since his mere
boyhood he had been dissatisfied with Hindúism, and
had sought for spiritual direction from the Mahratta
Bráhmans, amongst whom he had lived in Central
India, without finding any rest, or good hope that his
sins would be forgiven, through any course which they
directed him to pursue; that he had then practised
austerities under the direction of some faqírs, who
lived on Mount A'bú, with the same want of success;
that he had then attached himself to some Mohammedan faqírs, and found no relief under their direction; and that latterly he had been wandering as
chance led him, in the hope that he should find some
one to show him the right way. Then, he said, this
morning, when I saw your chapel open, and one or
two going in, I also went in; and you were just stating how Christ, by the sacrifice of himself, had laid
the ground for the full pardon of all who believe,
and lives and reigns now to intercede for and govern
his people; and that our own righteousness can never
do us any good, while his is perfect. It came into
my heart at once, "This is the righteousness that you
need: you know how long you have tried to gain
righteousness, and cannot—and here it can be given
to you. This is what you want." On further con-
versing with him, I thought he appeared more like an
apostolic convert than any one I had ever seen; he
seemed so entirely humble, and perfectly sensible that
he was a ruined and helpless sinner, and appeared
able to see through the doctrine of substitution so
clearly; his love of God and Christ seemed so simple, grateful and childlike; and his past ignorance of
the gospel seemed so complete, while his ready acqui-
escence in its statements was accompanied with such

21

admiring wonder and joy, that the Bábú and I could scarcely refrain from tears. We kept him with us, and instructed him. We found that, though a Mahratta, he could understand Hindí very well, and had no difficulty in reading it, because both languages are usually written in the Sanscrit character. A gentleman authorized me to give him four rupees a month as a subsistence allowance on his account, till we should see what he would prove to be. He remained with us about six weeks, and read industriously, attending all our religious services, both social and public. At the end of that time, when the cool season was just setting in, he came to me in the morning and asked for a month's allowance in advance, to enable him to get a padded cotton surcoat for winter, and said that he was going down to the city to get it. He then borrowed a fine suit of winter clothing, which had just been purchased by one of the young men in the printing-house, giving him the same account of what he intended to do, and started for the city. *We never saw or heard of him afterwards.* We debated many questions about him, with no result. Had he been a hypocrite all the time? His disappearance with the money and borrowed clothes looked like it. But if so, where did he get the knowledge of Christianity that enabled him to play his game in such an exquisitely perfect manner? If he was a true man, what became of him? Was it not possible that he fell into the hands of Thugs, or some other class of robbers, and was put out of the way? Mysterious disappearances from such causes were not at all uncommon formerly, though less frequent lately. Our general impression was, that he was a thief; but while we were thus blaming him, perhaps he was gone a saint—perhaps a martyr—to glory. It is not likely that we shall ever, in this world, learn more of this chapter of my experience.

One of the members of our church at Allahabad is

the son of a Mohammedan gentleman, who is the head of one of the twelve sacred families of that city. The father had long been in the habit of cultivating the acquaintance of English gentlemen; and when our mission was formed at that place he made our acquaintance. We talked much with him, and were the means of convincing him of the truth of Christianity. His son was introduced to us by him, and soon wished to profess our religion. The father made no objection, and the son was received. The father often proposed being baptized; but as often as he did so, he had some scruple, or made some difficulty, that hindered the affair. At one time he objected to sitting at the communion-table, on account of two or three of our members, who had been low caste Hindús. At another, he objected to the use of wine at the communion, because he had never used it, and feared it would make him sick. At another, he said his baptism must be in private, and kept secret, because he was afraid he should be murdered by his relatives. And at another time he said he would be baptized, if we would allow his body to be buried by his Mohammedan friends, and as that of a Mohammedan; because he was descended from kings, and was far too noble to lie down with the indiscriminate mob of the dead in a Christian burying-ground. We faithfully and affectionately met his objections, teaching him as he needed; and he often appeared so well, giving up his objections, that we were frequently on the point of baptizing him; but then he would always stay proceedings by some new fancy, or by the exhibition of something unchristian in his disposition. After he had passed several years in this way, he at last came to the conclusion that Christ would receive and save him without baptism; saying that he was only nominally a Musalmán, and was known by all not to practise any Musalmán rites, and to believe in Christ. He is old and somewhat childish now; and how far the decay of his intellect, and the power of his former prejudices, may have caused true faith to be imperfect in its action and development, we cannot tell. I saw him when last in Allahabad, and exhorted him to become a Christian. He answered me, with a smile, "I am a Christian." He had come to see me at considerable inconvenience to himself, being old and sick; and showed a good deal of affection for me and my family.

A few years since I formed an acquaintance with a lawyer, practising in the courts at Allahabad, on the occasion of having some business in one of the courts as treasurer of the mission. Out of our business connection grew up a considerable acquaintance and intimacy between the lawyer and our catechists; and we talked with him about Christianity. After I left Allahabad for Agra his intimacy with our people and my successor continued, and I heard that he was near making a profession of our religion. But when I came down again, on my way home, he came to see me, and showed me his doubts about the divinity of Christ and the inspiration of Paul's epistles. I know not how he had imbibed such doubts. We conversed together about three hours, and I tried to settle him in the faith, but not with decided success. He seemed to me to be completely converted *from* Mohammedanism, but not *to* Christianity; though he appeared devout and honest. The last that I knew of him was, that he remained suspended in doubt, but still under instruction. It is probable that his self-conceit as an intellectual and learned man, and perhaps his vanity as an acute disputant, hindered him from a full reception of the truth.

Our brethren at Saharunpore have had an interesting case of a convert from a village near that place, whose baptism was delayed till he was taken sick, when he caused himself to be brought to them, and would have been baptized, had not they thought that the natives would say, that they had improperly wrought upon him to receive the ordinance when he was senseless or imbecile. He died professing faith in Christ, and his family and connections are still well disposed towards us.

There are other persons, whose cases illustrate the fact that our doctrines are spreading and becoming influential. There are some who believe, and yet do not become personally acquainted with any missionary, and have not the opportunity to learn anything about the way of confessing Christ before men. There may be many hidden ones here and there, who have not access to any church, and do not know the usual mode of proceeding after believing. An instance of this kind is noticed in the fifth chapter, in the account of the fair of 1850; and another in a letter quoted from a friend. A young man of my acquaintance recently died at Allahabad confessing Christ earnestly, though he had not had decision enough to give up all for Christ by joining us. I knew a debating society of Hindús at Agra, who opened their meetings with prayer in the name of Christ, and wrote their performances on the basis of Christian truth, though none of them were yet prepared to lose all for Christ.

Our churches have received considerable accessions from the orphan asylums. These institutions have been very useful. They were formed during and immediately after the great famine of 1837. These asylums are accounted for in Chapter III, on the printing-house. From these all the churches have received accessions, and the native Christian communities are much enlarged by them. Many of these people are now married, and are raising up families in our connection. These asylums have preached loudly to the heathen. The benevolence that gathered and sustains them has been a beautiful proof of the kind spirit of Christianity. They are therefore most

21*

important. Some of our native assistant preachers
have come from them. All the members of communities, that have been raised up in them, have been
entirely separated from all native castes, and have no
interests conflicting with their Christian relations.
Too much ought not to be expected of them; for the
bad health that results from their early privations,
and the helplessness of character that often is produced by such a secluded education, operate as hinderances to their usefulness. But the valuable labours
and influence of many of them, the nuclei they form
for communities, and the improvement in their children, are advantages gained, that ought to be estimated
highly in an account of our success.

A sign that our doctrines are producing an effect
upon the country, is found in the fact, that works of
controversy against them have been called forth. The
Mohammedans and Hindús would never have written
against us, had they not seen that there was a danger
to their systems, to be averted if possible. The Mohammedans have produced many works, the greater
part of which are against the Christian views as to the
Godhead, and the authenticity of our Scriptures. One
of these books enters very largely into an exhibition
of alleged discrepancies of Scripture; and to make
these appear as numerous as possible, the author takes
up our different translations, together with the Persian
and Arabic ones, and takes the same verse from all,
giving his own interpretation of what each version
means, and so making the differences to appear as
great as the most strained and unfair treatment can
do. These works also bring forward other objections
to the Bible. The stories of Noah's intoxication, and
of Lot and his daughters, are treated as profane and
wicked slanders of prophets, and are said to be sure
indications that the book is not the true and original
book of God, but a corruption of it. They also allege
that there were prophecies of Mohammed as the last

of the prophets, which we have erased from the Old and New Testaments; and thus they attempt to show, that although they do profess to believe in the Pentateuch, the Psalms, and the Gospel, they need not and ought not to allow our Bible to be of any force in controversy. These books have been answered, and several others written, attacking their systems. Our missions have produced some valuable books bearing on this controversy. The circulation of native books is rather limited.

The Hindús have made less attempts to defend their system in this way. One such was made at Benares, a few years ago. A young Pandit was induced by the Benares Bráhmans to stand forward as their champion, and write a refutation of the Bible; but his attempt resulted in his own conversion, and he is now a useful preacher of the gospel.

Much has been done for Christianity by schools. All our mission stations have schools of various kinds. There are small vernacular schools, with Hindú teachers, in which Christian books are used, and which the missionaries visit as often as they can, to give them religious instruction. They also often make the places where these schools are kept, stands for preaching. Many boys that are brought up in these little schools remain our firm friends, and the most intelligent hearers of preaching amongst the common classes of natives. I have several times been befriended and supported in my efforts in the bázárs, by former pupils in our schools. Every station also has its central school, in which English and science are taught, as well as the vernacular.

Lately there has grown up a feeling, in certain quarters in America, that missionaries ought not to engage at all in giving instruction in secular knowledge, but ought to confine themselves to the direct preaching of the gospel. This agitation I regret; for popular excitements are always liable to proceed too far. If this movement should result in the destruction of schools, instead of being confined to the correction of occasional abuses, it will be evil. I have never been engaged in teaching a native school to such an extent as at all to identify me personally with them, or give any bias to my convictions on this point; and therefore I may claim to be a better judge of the policy of teaching than a professed teacher would be allowed to be; and better, perhaps, than those who have had less, or no opportunities for extended personal observation. First, then, the teaching of a school does not usually, and ought never to hinder a missionary from preaching. Whoever has read my chapters on preaching at the stations, and itinerating, will perceive that a missionary who teaches a few hours in the day, may still have the morning and the evening for street and chapel preaching. If any neglect this branch of their labour, they should be dealt with as individuals, and brought to their duty. To abolish the schools would be a poor remedy, and probably not a successful one. A man who will not preach when he has the opportunity, should be recalled. The teacher may, and ought to, spend his winter vacation in itinerating. The schools ought to be so arranged that the missionary should not be employed in teaching more than two or three hours daily; and then he would have no excuse for not preaching at least once a day. The schoolroom is as good a preaching-place as any other. Indeed it affords more facilities than the street. We here retain the same audience through many successive occasions, and thus have a better opportunity to enforce and illustrate the truth; while in the street we have the most fluctuating attendance. Not that the street ought to be forsaken for the school; and, equally, the school ought not to be abolished for the sake of the street— especially when both can be attended to as well as either alone.

Secondly, it is a fact that no instruction can be

given to Hindús on such matters as geography and astronomy, without proving to them the falsehood of some of their sacred books, and showing them most clearly the absurdity of some of their religious dogmas. And if the missionaries do not teach them, they leave them so much under the influence of their pandits, whose power is, to a great extent, founded on their supposed knowledge of these matters. Not to teach, is to surrender the use of powerful weapons to our adversaries. And if the reader will refer to my remarks on the importance of a Christian literature, contained in the chapter on the preparation of books, he will see the importance and necessity of our teaching history, in order to prepare the native mind for the reception of the evidences of our religion. I do not mean to limit the power of God's grace, which can produce conviction in any circumstances; but still I am writing on the principle that means ought to be adapted to produce the end desired.

Another reason for giving secular instruction is, that it benefits the people; and it is the work of Christianity to practise all kinds of beneficence. One of the most powerful objections to Christianity, which are ignorantly brought forward by infidels, is, that it is all for the soul, and nothing for the body; and the best answer that can be given to the objection is, to point to the schools and hospitals, and similar institutions, that exist almost exclusively in Christian lands. Now, the natives of Hindustan see the benign nature of our religion in the schools that we support and teach; and thus these institutions actually preach—sometimes with a more distinct and forcible utterance than could be employed by their teachers in any other capacity.

The last that I heard of the mission-school at Allahabad, it had six hundred scholars on its roll, and the roll was purged every month of all names marked absent during the whole previous month. The mis-

sionary at the head of that school can give a lecture
every morning on the passage of Scripture read,
which will be understood and appreciated by about
half of the school—a far larger audience than he could
usually gain in the town. He can teach Bible lessons
to the higher classes; his native Christian teachers
do the same to the lower classes; the pupils all learn
Scripture history and the evidences of Christianity;
and the whole powerful influence of the institution is
in favour of the truth.

" *Whatsoever* thy hand findeth to do, do it with
thy might." We ought to use all the instruments
of doing good; and in such proportions and combinations as shall accomplish the greatest amount of good.
We ought to preach and teach, to write and print.
Why is it necessary that contending for one thing
that is right should set us against another thing that
is also right? Ultraism is no more proper in regard
to the duty of direct preaching than in anything else.

The East India Company supports several colleges
for the education of the natives. Until recently the
teachers in these colleges were forbidden to teach
Christianity. Now there is guarded liberty to use
the Bible in the instruction of pupils who do not object to it. The influence of these schools is in favour
of the demolition of the native superstitions, and is so
far good. The government has also determined to
aid private and missionary schools under certain conditions. These improvements in the efforts of the
government to promote sound education must be attributed, in some measure, to the influence of missions.
The mission schools have triumphantly shown that
there is no danger resulting from teaching the Scriptures, and also that schools will not be deserted
because of their introduction. These schools, the
railroads and telegraphs, and other influences that are
brought to bear on India, give hope that some great
changes are impending; and the Church ought to

seize her full share of the influence to be exerted, and hold herself in readiness to use every future opportunity.

It would not be right to close this part of my work without making a plea for the country in which I have so long lived and laboured; and if it were not appropriate, still my feelings would impel me to it. We have seen that the people need the gospel; that we have liberty, protection and health to a good degree while proclaiming it; that the people are accessible; that a great part of the preparatory work has been done, and a great many influences aid us; and that thousands are prepared, so far as knowledge is concerned, to be made the subjects of converting grace, if the Spirit of God were poured out upon them. The word is the instrument of the Spirit. That instrument is there present. It does not merely lie in books, but also in the minds of thousands of the people: they know enough to be wrought upon without further preparation, or any further miracle than is performed in every conversion from sin to holiness.

If this be true, then the time is come that the Church should pray, with more earnestness and fervour than ever before, for the outpouring of the Spirit of God upon India, and upon all fields similarly white to the harvest. This is the great want of the present time. Prayer is more restrained than contributions or personal effort. There is not enough of either; but Christians seem more ready to give and labour than to accompany their gifts with earnest, agonizing prayer, that God would follow them with his blessing. The formality, the brevity, and the cold tone of prayers offered for the heathen, together with the small attendance at missionary prayer-meetings, show that this is true. Christians lack enlarged thoughts and high aspirations in behalf of the cause of Christ. They feel less than they ought for either Christ, the Church, or for souls. From want of feeling, belief, though real, becomes low and uninfluential; and the prayer-meeting, which relates to things so little felt and appreciated, languishes; the petitions for the heathen become everywhere few, and are crowded into the end of the prayer, where they ought not to be, if Christ arranged the subjects of prayer properly when he taught his disciples to pray. The meeting thus becomes a burdensome ceremony; and it is no wonder that the smallest excuses serve to keep people away. So it happens that when Christians are assembled to pray about our Saviour's very last command, and may think that they have a clear right to expect the special fulfilment of the promise that accompanies it, then it is that He seems least of all present with them. This, surely, is not his fault. If our services were of the right character, we should not lack his presence. If we felt as we ought about the cause of Christ, we should be drawn to the place of prayer; we should go to pour out desires that would not be restrained; we should seek there the exercise and relief of overpowering affections. Then Christ would keep his promise to us; and we have no right to it otherwise. If we prepare the altar, the wood, and the offering, he will be sure to send down the fire from heaven.

Then let us pray that the Holy Spirit may do his part of the work of conversion—the indispensable and only efficient part—in the hearts of the multitudes whom we have taught in the cities, in the villages and by the wayside, in the schools and by the press. The seed lies in their minds. The Holy Spirit can cause it to germinate, and send its roots all through their hearts. God waits to be gracious: for these things he will be inquired of by us, to do them for us. Shall these enlightened heathens die, with the unfruitful seed in their hearts, to spring up and bring forth the fruit of eternal remorse hereafter, because we will not take up a position which God can bless consistently with his glory? It is a dreadful thought, that after all that has been done for the heathen, *we* should be the occasion of the crowning mercy being withheld from them. Let us learn to pray for Christ and his kingdom first, before we ask for daily bread or any other mercy to ourselves.

If the Spirit were poured out on our missions in answer to prayer, and the intelligence were to come over, month after month, of souls pressing into the kingdom, what an impulse would be given to all that is good here! How faith would be strengthened, and love and zeal warmed, and efforts redoubled, and a blessed revival be secured even here, that would fully show that "he that watereth, shall himself be watered."

22

CONCLUSION.

THERE are many other topics which a book on India might embrace, but the object proposed in the writing of this work does not necessarily include them. Many readers may have expected to see more on two subjects; that is, on the nature and doctrines of Hindúism, and on the character of the Hindús. The first of these topics has not been treated of, in a formal manner, chiefly because other works are accessible, which give a sufficient idea of it. And if any reader has not access to such works, he may learn from the incidental statements of this, a great many of its practices and much of its spirit. Further, a particular description if its deities, its rites, and its sects, could not be brought into the compass of a book smaller than this. Less would tell scarcely more than may be gathered from what is already in this volume. And, after all, the great thing that Christians need to know in this case, is the mournful fact, that there are thirty-five millions of people, within the field of our North India mission, who are following idols and Mohammed, and are under the influence of systems that lead them as directly and completely away from God as the arch-enemy of mankind could desire. Although they are, after a certain manner, a civilized people, yet they are as far from the truth as fetichism carries the people of Africa. This ought to be enough to excite the pity of all Christians; and if it will not do so in some cases, neither would the most detailed statement of Hindú doctrines do so. The character of the people of North India, also, may be sufficiently gathered from this work, without a formal dissertation on the subject. There is only one essential matter that, on review, appears to the writer to have been neglected, which it is necessary to his design to add.

The races that inhabit North India are the chief races of India in every point of view. It is the home of the Bráhman, the Rájpút, the Sikh, and the most valuable classes of the lower castes of Hindús.

All history shows that this part of India has always been its head and heart. Here were the great kingdoms of the Hindús. From this place went out the influences that formed all the systems of Central and Southern India. If those systems differ now from those of the north, it is only where the effeminacy of the south has operated to make Hindúism more lascivious and ferocious. The Rome of Hindúism is in the north—Benares. The great bathing places are all in the north—Allahabad, Hardwar, and the source of the Ganges. The holy land of Hindúism is in the north—the region about Mutthra. The chief and holiest Bráhmans, the head of the Kulíns of Bengal, are in the north—the Kanauj Bráhmans. Musalmán Empire had its strength in the north, and from thence reached forth its long and strong arms all over the peninsula. The English army of Bengal is wholly recruited from the north—no soldiers are raised in Bengal proper. One who travels from Calcutta to the northwest will notice, after reaching Patna, that every day's march brings him amongst men of greater physical and mental vigour and stamina, and of more and more independence and manliness.

How immeasurably important then, is it that this part of the Indian field should be diligently and abundantly cultivated. If this were Christian, the Hindúism of other portions would have no standing-ground. Influences of a right kind would go forth from the region, which all the rest of India has always been accustomed to follow. And we stand, as it were, at the very foot of the roads that lead into western China, Thibet, Afghánistán and all the countries of central Asia. If North India were Christian, what influences would spread from it, literally radiating over the darkest and most hopeless portions of Asia! When a Christian is acquainted with history, understands the position and character of North India, and spreads out the map of Asia before him, so that he can see what grand movements our mission may be initiating, it is enough to fire his soul with courage, perseverance and zeal.

THE END.

Trieste

Trieste Publishing has a massive catalogue of classic book titles. Our aim is to provide readers with the highest quality reproductions of fiction and non-fiction literature that has stood the test of time. The many thousands of books in our collection have been sourced from libraries and private collections around the world.

The titles that Trieste Publishing has chosen to be part of the collection have been scanned to simulate the original. Our readers see the books the same way that their first readers did decades or a hundred or more years ago. Books from that period are often spoiled by imperfections that did not exist in the original. Imperfections could be in the form of blurred text, photographs, or missing pages. It is highly unlikely that this would occur with one of our books. Our extensive quality control ensures that the readers of Trieste Publishing's books will be delighted with their purchase. Our staff has thoroughly reviewed every page of all the books in the collection, repairing, or if necessary, rejecting titles that are not of the highest quality. This process ensures that the reader of one of Trieste Publishing's titles receives a volume that faithfully reproduces the original, and to the maximum degree possible, gives them the experience of owning the original work.

We pride ourselves on not only creating a pathway to an extensive reservoir of books of the finest quality, but also providing value to every one of our readers. Generally, Trieste books are purchased singly - on demand, however they may also be purchased in bulk. Readers interested in bulk purchases are invited to contact us directly to enquire about our tailored bulk rates. Email: customerservice@triestepublishing.com

You May Also Like

Persecution and Tolerance: Being the Hulsean Lectures Preached Before the University of Cambridge in 1893-4

Mandell Creighton

ISBN: 9780649669356
Paperback: 164 pages
Dimensions: 6.14 x 0.35 x 9.21 inches
Language: eng

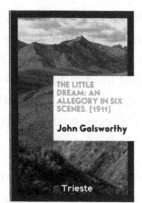

The Little Dream: An Allegory in Six Scenes. [1911]

John Galsworthy

ISBN: 9780649637270
Paperback: 50 pages
Dimensions: 6.14 x 0.10 x 9.21 inches
Language: eng

www.triestepublishing.com

You May Also Like

ISBN: 9780649724185
Paperback: 130 pages
Dimensions: 6.14 x 0.28 x 9.21 inches
Language: eng

Report of the Second Annual Meeting of the Maryland State Bar Association, Held at Ocean City, Maryland, July 28-29, 1897

Conway W. Sams

ISBN: 9780649057054
Paperback: 140 pages
Dimensions: 6.14 x 0.30 x 9.21 inches
Language: eng

The University of Minnesota. The Calendar for the Year 1883-84

University Minneapolis

You May Also Like

ISBN: 9780649420544
Paperback: 108 pages
Dimensions: 6.14 x 0.22 x 9.21 inches
Language: eng

1807-1907 The One Hundredth Anniversary of the incorporation of the Town of Arlington Massachusetts

Various

ISBN: 9780649194292
Paperback: 44 pages
Dimensions: 6.14 x 0.09 x 9.21 inches
Language: eng

Biennial report of the Board of State Harbor Commissioners, for the two fiscal years commencing July 1, 1890, and ending June 30, 1892

Various

You May Also Like

ISBN: 9780649199693
Paperback: 48 pages
Dimensions: 6.14 x 0.10 x 9.21 inches
Language: eng

Biennial report of the Board of State Harbor Commissioners for the two fisca years. Commeneing July 1, 1884, and Ending June 30, 1886

Various

ISBN: 9780649196395
Paperback: 44 pages
Dimensions: 6.14 x 0.09 x 9.21 inches
Language: eng

Biennial report of the Board of state commissioners, for the two fiscal years, commencing July 1, 1890, and ending June 30, 1892

Various

Find more of our titles on our website. We have a selection of thousands of titles that will interest you. Please visit

www.triestepublishing.com

Lightning Source UK Ltd.
Milton Keynes UK
UKOW06f1511231017
311488UK00007B/1851/P